Jane Kennedy

Jane Kennedy

Fabulous food, minus the boombah

hardie grant books

MELBOURNE · LONDON

Published in 2009 by
Hardie Grant Books
85 High Street
Prahran, Victoria 3181, Australia
www.hardiegrant.com.au
www.hardiegrant.co.uk

Cataloguing-in-Publication data is available from the
National Library of Australia.

ISBN 978 1 74066 808 8

Edited by Lucy Malouf
Photography by Mark Roper
Food styling by Deborah Kaloper
Propping by Leesa O'Reilly
Design by Trisha Garner
Colour reproduction by Splitting Image Colour Studio
Printed and bound in China by 1010 Printing International Limited

The publisher would like to thank the following for their generosity
in supplying props for the book: Craft Victoria, Country Road,
Empire Vintage, The Essential Ingredient, Hun Furniture Lighting
Living, Izzi & Popo, Make Design Objects, Manon Bis, Market
Import and Safari Living.

10 9 8 7 6 5 4 3 2

To Mum, Dad and Carrie:
Thank you for teaching me to love life and food.

To Rob, Mia, Josh, Maxy, Bailey and Andy:
I love our circus.

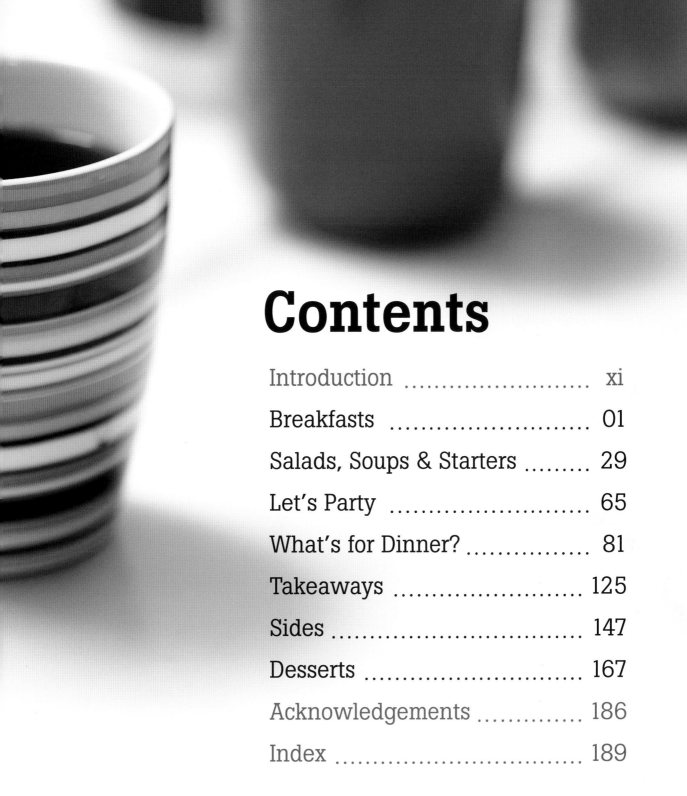

Contents

Boombah: (adj)
Word to describe food that
makes your arse huge.

Introduction

I love food. Always have. Unfortunately I love it about one kilo per month more than I should. Perhaps I should put it another way: the food I love seems to have more calories than I need and over a month and a year and a lifetime ... it adds up! Yep, I get FAT.

I reluctantly came to the conclusion that there was only one way to get that calorie equation in sync with my desire to wear Bettina Liano jeans: strip the food I eat of all flavour, pretend a handful of carrots constitutes a meal and accept being peckish for the foreseeable future.

But that's just not fair. And it's not fun. And food *should* be fun *and* it should be delicious. This book came from that notion. It's based on the belief that there HAS to be a middle ground, and has emerged from dozens, if not hundreds, of attempts to create really tasty food that didn't add a dress size. Food WITH flavour and WITHOUT THE BOOMBAH!

The battle started early for me. I was pretty pudgy as a kid. I ate too much and was disinterested in sport. In fact, I was the classic girl, feigning every disease to get out of sports day. Then, to my delight, I got glandular fever. This effectively shut my gob for months. It was simply too painful to eat my normal buttered crumpets with salami and cheese (a usual after-school snack). So by the time I returned to school, I'd lost a stack of weight. I also found that now (as the laws of physics were working for me), I wanted to play sport. Even though I was pretty average, I took to the netball court and loved it.

Unfortunately, old habits die hard. The crumpets came back and so did the kilos ... just like long-lost friends. And so, over the next ten years my weight yo-yo'd.

Then I moved out of home. This is an important time in a girl's life, a time when she discovers the freedom to order takeaway food every night of the week. I have great memories of watching John Hughes videos with my girlfriends and ordering something called 'Los trios dips with corn chips' from a local Mexican restaurant ... repeatedly. I'd get heavier and exercise would just seem like, well, exercise until I'd eventually realise that I was porking up. I could take a number of approaches. I generally settled on the most logical option: the latest fad diet.

My Diet Hall of Fame includes quite a few corkers:

The Israeli Army Diet, which consists of eating four items over eight days: two days of apples, two days of cheese, two days of chicken, two days of salad. I lasted two days.

The Scarsdale Diet Start each day with grapefruit to get your 'fat-eating' enzymes working, eat a tin of tuna for lunch and unlimited lean meat for dinner. The benefit of this is that it allegedly produces ketosis in the body. The same ketosis that causes alcoholics and diabetics to rapidly lose weight as an unwanted side-effect of their disease. SPOOKY BELLS! Get me a pizza. Lasted one day.

Diet replacement drinks Those cans of powder used as a meal replacement? Yep, I tried them. A shake for breakfast, shake for lunch. Hello, I'm hungry! (Does eighteen hours count as a day?)

The Beverly Hills Diet This fad shouted 'Instant results' – lose weight the same way Hollywood starlets do. Unfortunately, they forgot to list the most important ingredient for weight loss in Hollywood: cocaine. No joy there.

Calorie-controlled home-delivered meals Yep, a week's worth of food delivered to your door, in calorie-controlled packs. The food arrived on Monday. I'd eaten the lot by Wednesday. Oooops.

Starvation and fags My most successful, if temporary, weight loss back then was when I was acting in a comedy series set in the '70s and faced wearing a wardrobe of vintage clothes. *Tiny* vintage clothes. I couldn't get one leg in some of those jeans. But I was desperate to wear them so I turned to the number-one diet go-to for chicks: I stopped eating and smoked a thousand cigarettes. That, combined with a hundred cups of black coffee a day, sure dropped those boombah pounds.*

Again I found myself on the diet merry-go-round, resigned to the fact that I had to eat bowls of lettuce with no dressing, steamed fish and something called quinoa. God, it was BORING.

Years went by and I was always resorting to some extreme measure. Oh, and what joy! My career at the time involved appearing on camera. Well the bloke who designed the TV camera forgot about inventing a switch to stop adding seven kilos every time you appeared on screen. Thanks for that!

When I started having children, I gave myself permission to eat for two. It's the time when you don't notice you've put on weight because it's the baby … right? Yippee! Bring on the milkshakes, the bowls of creamy risotto and macaroni cheese. Crumpets … welcome back. Unless my first baby had a birth weight of a small teenager, the twenty kilos I added was mostly *my* doing.

I wasn't trying to qualify as a story on *A Current Affair* but I ended up having five children in five years (a set of twins will do that). So for half a decade, my body shape resembled a piano accordion, inflating and deflating after every

---

*Small point: somewhere along the way I turned into a superbitch. Sure, I looked okay in the clothes but I was starving. I was horrid and cranky – no one wanted to be near me – and as soon as we wrapped the final show I jumped in my car, made a beeline for the nearest drive thru and ate forty-seven Big Macs. Suffice to say, I put the weight back on.

delivery. And that's where I ended up, back at square one: overweight, staring down a year of chicken consommé dinners, and with no 'wow-the-weight-just-fell-off-me-when-I-breastfed' miracle awaiting.

I finally grew a brain and motivated myself to see a personal trainer (thank you, Donna). Without a spring in my step. Exercise was hard! And here's the bad news: my trainer always says that exercise alone will NOT make you lose weight. You have to watch what goes in your gob. Groan. Well, here is my big whinge: Why is diet food so BORING? It's impossible to stick to a meal plan that reads: 'Dinner – one small piece of steak, unlimited steamed vegies.' Even buying the ingredients makes me slightly depressed. No fun for you tonight, honey! I slowly realised that if I was going to lose weight, somehow I had to fight flavour with flavour.

FLAVOUR

For the most part, this has become the 'boombah' bit in food: the fatty, creamy, crispy, sugary combination that sends a signal to our brains that we're eating something delicious. Boombah has taken over. Especially in restaurants and food outlets. Chefs aren't stupid. If they double the cream they double the compliments! Well done. But the world of non-boombah flavours has taken a backseat. So here are the ingredients that I turn to for that flavour hit.

Chillies Food flavoured with chilli transports your tastebuds. It needn't blow your head off; one small chilli is usually enough to elevate the plainest of dishes.

Limes Lime juice is NOT the same as lemon juice. Lime juice is instantly exotic and 'summery'. Its fresh, sour flavour can be dish-transforming.

Garlic There's a reason garlic is a staple of so many cuisines. It lifts everything it touches. It takes boring food and makes it brilliant.

Fresh herbs Not just parsley, please: think tarragon, dill, chervil, thyme, oregano, lemongrass, basil, coriander, rosemary. Taste them! Use them. Novelty alone will make the dish more interesting. They're all so different. Herbs change the way food tastes. They're the perfect boombah replacement.

Ginger As with garlic, ginger is warm, fragrant and a staple of Asian, Middle Eastern and African cuisines. *Always* have some in your bowl on the kitchen bench.

Kaffir lime leaves Why has it taken me so long to get onto these? Put simply, kaffir lime leaves make Asian food taste great. Add these to your green curries and you'll think you've moved to Bangkok.

Spices Another non-boombah winner. It's no mystery to me why Indian, Thai, Turkish and Moroccan food tastes so bloody good. Spices are the jewels that set these cuisines apart from the boring 'meat and three veg' world. Hello, what do you think the Spice Trade was all about? Those guys knew what they had. People killed for this stuff, yet you can get it at the 7-Eleven! Ground cumin and coriander, cinnamon and nutmeg, cardamom pods, mustard seeds, saffron and turmeric. Fenugreek is crazy – all I know is that if it's not in an Indian curry it doesn't taste the same. Take pride in your spice rack and refresh the spices every now and then. Five-year-old cumin will add NO flavour.

Peppercorns and sea salt Not pepper and salt. Real peppercorns and real sea salt. Freshly cracked pepper is one of the world's great cheats and sea salt is the world's *greatest* cheat. Use them.

Sesame seeds and nuts Texture is just so important in food, and a few peanuts or cashews or a sprinkle of toasted sesame seeds will give your food the 'crunch' you crave.

GOODBYE BORING DIET-FOOD WORLD

I'm a cookbook junkie. I read cookbooks instead of novels. But most of the 'tantalising' recipes in these books involve boombah, boombah and boombah. And that don't work for me. So, driven by the desire to eat the food I saw in the photos and armed with my 'invincible' cache of flavours, I decided to leave the boring diet-food world forever.

I set up my own laboratory, if you like, testing and tasting and seeing how much of the boombah I could take out while keeping the flavour. A non-boombah beef vindaloo? If you get rid of half the oil and stop serving it with a bucket of rice, then yeah! A Thai green curry? You bet! Remove the truckload of coconut milk and use a small amount for flavour – mmm, that's not bad.

There's another secret to enjoying appetising foods this way: portion size. We all eat too much (I know I did). Serving sizes of food have reached ridiculous proportions and you have to do something about it. Buy a set of kitchen scales. I'm not kidding. You gotta start weighing your food or you'll chumba wumba up. Meat, fish and chicken portions in the following recipes are between 120 and 140 grams. You've probably been used to eating 200 or 250 grams (or more!) of meat in one sitting. Many restaurants now boast about the size of their steaks ('Would you like that 500 g side of beef cooked medium-rare, sir?'). Well, I'm saying that's too much. We've all gone mad. Once you add lots of flavour and crunch from lettuce or vegetables and chilli or herbs, you'll cope with eating smaller meals.

This way of cooking and eating works for me (I know it works for guys too). I feel much healthier and happier and I've got a lot more energy (no need for that afternoon nanna nap). These recipes have to be better for you than chowing down on a creepy bowl of 2 minute noodles and an entire pack of Tim Tams (yes, it's time to let go). Be disciplined, even if you've struggled before. And if you really can't live without your nightly routine of creamy pasta with garlic bread or butter chicken with naan, then bung this book back on the shelf. But stop whingeing about your huge arse.

N.B. THE FOLLOWING CONTAINS ADVICE YOU MAY NOT WANT TO HEAR
(I'm still not sure I do)

'But I need my comfort food.' Mmmmm burger ... Oh, it makes everything better. Yeah right. To give yourself whatever 'comfort' you think you need, you scoff a load of creamy, fatty, crunchy whatever. And you DO feel better for a little while ... until you feel WORSE. Which is why I simply call comfort food DISCOMFORT food. You know what it is. Stop eating it.

'I don't have time to exercise/I'm just sooo busy.' You know that's crap. How come you've got the time for that haircut/colour/manicure/massage/brow wax/pilates/lunchwiththegirls? Make time to move your body. Who cares what your nails look like? Set your alarm clock early, get up before everyone else and go for a walk two to three times a week.

'I'm big-boned.' Rubbish. Your frame of bones might be larger, but how does that affect the not-so-solid bits around them? Those love handles have nothing to do with bones.

'It's hereditary.' Then break the chain! Your family just ate too much. Be the black sheep.

'People should just accept me for who I am.' We do. But do you? This is a big one. Your sensitive, walk-on-eggshells, defensive response is because you know damn well you'd love yourself more if you just committed to losing some of those unwanted kilos.

'I would eat healthily, but I can't cook.' What are you, a baby? Of course you can. Get a frying pan, turn on the heat, sprinkle some sea salt and pepper on a steak, rub on some olive oil, put the steak in the pan. Look, you cooked.

'It's too hard when I have to cook for the rest of the family.' Boo hoo. Ask your family to share the same meals. You'll be surprised at how supportive people can be, especially when the food tastes great. Really.

It's very hard to lose weight.

Accepted.

But now is the time to start feeling and looking the best you possibly can.

I'LL MAKE IT A LITTLE EASIER FOR YOU...

Buddy up. Grab a friend, partner, sister, mum or dad. Share meals, talk over recipes, weight and body changes, keep a food diary. Have a whinge to each other! Inspire each other.

In vino veritas. I do drink wine – I'm not completely mad. I have a glass while I'm cooking the kids' dinner (mental image, please: five kids under eight) and then I try to have only one more at 'grown-ups' dinner. But I pay for that indulgence ... wine is really fattening, as is most alcohol. Have a few alcohol-free days each week. I've always been too much of a baby to stop completely so my compromise is adding a couple of ice cubes to my six o'clock vino, just to make sure I don't overdo it.

I know, water's boring. So try these:

- Add half a fresh lime and its juice to an ice-filled tall glass of mineral or soda water.

- Throw a bunch of fresh mint leaves into a pot of boiling water and make the same peppermint tea you pay eight bucks for at your local bistro.

- Slice some fresh ginger into a mug of boiling water. It smells DIVINE.

It's been drummed into us for years and it's the truth. You must drink water. Not just one pissy glass. About two litres a day. Just do it, okay?

Get organised. The key to successful weight loss with this style of eating is to be organised. Disorganisation is the open door through which every second excuse (or french fry) slips. 'Oh no, the stores are closed. Oh well, better order takeaway.' Don't do it. *There. Is. No. Good. Takeaway. Food.* *

Chuck out your home-delivery menus. NOW.

WHAT TO HAVE IN YOUR PANTRY AND FRIDGE

This pantry section will probably look a little different from those in other cookbooks. Aside from a few oils and vinegars, mustards and cans of tomatoes, there's really not much in my own pantry. That's because all those cookies, sugary cereals, white rice, pasta, chips, noodle boxes and lollies are no good for us folk prone to 'boombahing–up'. Chuck 'em in the bin. As Dr Phil says, 'Remove temptation'.

'But what about all the stuff I have to have for the kids in the cupboard? I can't throw that out.' Okay, I don't expect your kids to stop eating sandwiches and cereals and

*Unless you meant a small serving of fresh sashimi. But that's not what you meant, is it?

spaghetti, cos mine still do. Here's my solution: the pantry is divided into 'my side' and 'their side'. (Why would you want to eat a brightly coloured cupcake anyway? What are you, six years old?)

All *you* need should be in your fridge or your herb garden. (Yes, you will have one.)

Changing the way you eat shouldn't cost a fortune, and gathering the ingredients doesn't take time or effort. I'm not suggesting you suddenly join a food co-op or attend famers' markets religiously. Nearly every one of the following ingredients can be found at a convenience store. Here's what I always have on hand, to avoid the temptation to veer into boombah territory:

extra-virgin olive oil
sesame oil
light soy sauce
wasabi
Worcestershire sauce
balsamic vinegar
horseradish cream
Dijon mustard
seeded mustard
hot English mustard
canned tomatoes
whole egg mayonnaise
marinated goat's cheese
Greek yoghurt
parmesan cheese
free-range eggs
bacon
ham
tomatoes
continental cucumbers
rocket

red and white onions
zucchini
asparagus
snow peas
capsicums
spring onions
lemons
limes
chillies
garlic
ginger
fresh herbs
kaffir lime leaves (they freeze really well, just pop them in a plastic bag)
pepper
sea salt
spices
a few steaks (which you can freeze)
some skinless chicken fillets (also to freeze)

HOW DOES YOUR HERB GARDEN GROW?

Herbs will help you de-boombah your life. It's so easy to have fresh herbs on hand, either potted or planted, and they'll be the basis of nearly every meal you prepare. Rosemary grows like crazy (and besides lamb, it goes brilliantly with fish), you can't kill mint (or is that just me?), and more seasonal herbs like basil and coriander are pretty straightforward.

I built my herb wall from pots and plants bought at a hardware superstore. It's a very impressive look when you just grab a handful of herbs from your own garden and throw them into your dish. And if you can't grow your own, most grocery stores now stock packets of parsley, coriander and basil.

KITCHEN NOTES

When I refer to olive oil, I mean extra-virgin olive oil. I buy big tins of imported olive oil, usually on special, and just keep refilling a large glass bottle with a cork pourer I got from a discount shop. This way you can keep everything handy – don't put the oil, pepper, salt or lemons away. They *must* stay out.

Salt is always sea salt (Maldon or Murray River pink salt).

Pepper is always freshly ground pepper, unless stated otherwise.

Mayonnaise is always good quality egg-based mayonnaise, like Best's.

Greek yoghurt is always the thick natural yoghurt found in supermarkets.

You will need a Microplane grater, a good non-stick frying pan, a heavier based ovenproof frying pan that can be transferred from stove to oven, at least one really sharp knife and some good white platters. You might want to get a couple of square white dinner plates – somehow, food looks more impressive (and filling) on a square plate. If you don't believe me, try it!

So let's say goodbye to boombah.
Go for it! And *enjoy!*

Breakfasts

I'm not going to kid you, changing the way you eat breakfast is not easy. Cereals, toast, crumpets, pancakes (get the picture?) can't be part of your life anymore. Those carbs are so hard to burn off, and the spreads you add to them load up the calories too.

Big deal. There are plenty of wonderful breakfast alternatives. I'm not suggesting you eat seven omelettes a week, but the fact is, eggs are a seriously efficient and versatile form of protein. And they are filling and satisfying – which means you won't be eyeing off a muffin at morning tea.

So how about serving spicy huevos rancheros eggs for breakfast one morning? Or have you thought about trying watermelon and tangy feta? Or a warming bowl of porridge with sweet blueberries? Feeling better about breakfast?

Bacon-wrapped baked eggs

This is a cool way to serve bacon and eggs. The bacon wraps around the egg like flower petals as it cooks. Alternatively, you can wait for the dish to cool, slip it out of the ramekin and eat it cold.

1 teaspoon butter

2 rashers bacon

2 eggs

salt and freshly ground pepper

1 tablespoon freshly snipped chives

Preheat the oven to 200°C and butter the insides of 2 x 150 ml ramekins. Line the inside of each with a rasher of bacon and place in the oven for 5 minutes. Remove from the oven and crack an egg into each ramekin. Season with salt and pepper and return to the oven for 7–8 minutes, or until the egg whites are set.

Remove from oven and sprinkle with fresh chives as you serve.

SERVES 2

Huevos rancheros (Mexican eggs)

Hang on to those ramekins! These are not really traditional huevos rancheros eggs, because, well, you don't need oily tortilla or sour cream or black beans to ruin your morning. This is my version, which is lighter and less stodgy. It's best to use wide ramekins for this dish or the egg white will spill over onto the tomato mixture.

1 tablespoon olive oil
½ white onion, finely chopped
1 clove garlic, finely chopped
1 green capsicum, finely chopped
1 x 400 g can chopped tomatoes
½ teaspoon chilli powder
½ teaspoon ground cumin
½ teaspoon dried oregano
salt and freshly ground pepper
4 eggs
¼ cup grated parmesan cheese
1–2 spring onions, finely chopped

Preheat the oven to 200°C.

Heat the olive oil in a non-stick frying pan over a medium heat and sauté the onion, garlic and capsicum for 1 minute. Add the tomatoes, chilli, cumin and oregano and season with salt and pepper.

Divide the tomato sauce between 4 x 250 ml ramekins, so they are about three-quarters full. Make a deep indentation in the sauce and carefully crack an egg into each. Sprinkle with cheese and spring onion and bake for about 10 minutes, or until the eggs are set. Serve straight away.

SERVES 4

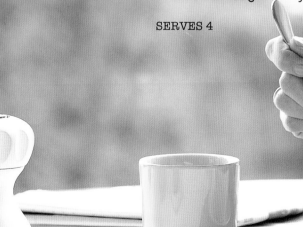

Scrambled eggs with tomato and Tabasco

This will become a standby flash-fast breakfast. The kick of Tabasco lifts this dish from plain to perky.

1 teaspoon butter
½ tomato, chopped
2 spring onions, chopped
Tabasco to taste
2 eggs, lightly whisked
salt and freshly ground pepper
sprinkle of freshly chopped flat-leaf parsley

Melt the butter in a non-stick frying pan over a medium heat. Add the tomato and spring onions and stir for about 1 minute. Add a few shakes of Tabasco to the eggs and tip into the pan. Stir gently until the egg just starts to set. Season with salt and pepper, sprinkle with parsley and serve immediately.

SERVES 1

Smoked salmon, rocket and cream cheese

Here's another savoury breakfast idea that seems more indulgent than it actually is.

For each person, simply spread a thin layer of low-fat cream cheese onto 3 slices of smoked salmon, add some soft, fresh baby rocket leaves and roll up like sushi. Serve with lemon juice and freshly ground pepper.

Omelette in a flash

Did you see the movie *Big Night*? I love the final scene where Stanley Tucci's character makes a simple omelette on screen in real time. It takes two and a half minutes and no words are spoken. He adds no more than a pinch of salt, but do feel free to add a small handful of shredded ham, chopped mushrooms or tomatoes to the pan before adding the egg mixture.

This is how I make my omelettes.

½ tablespoon olive oil
2 eggs
pinch of sea salt

Heat the oil in a non-stick frying pan over a high heat. Whisk the eggs with a fork and add a pinch of salt. Lower the heat and add the eggs to the pan. Swirl the mixture around with a non-stick spatula until the omelette settles – it will take about 30 seconds. Cook for a further minute, then fold the omelette in half, slide it out of the pan and serve immediately.

SERVES 1

A couple of frittatas

I guess in the past we ate quiche ... but quiche
is BOOMBAH! These days frittata is our friend.
It's lighter, just as tasty and 'easy as' to make.
In fact, it's so good, you almost feel like you're
cheating!

Salmon and spinach frittata

This frittata is filling and full of flavour. I know it's more gourmet to use fresh smoked salmon, but I really think it tastes better with salmon from the can.

3 eggs

2 egg whites

1 tablespoon Greek yoghurt

½ cup grated parmesan cheese

½ tablespoon finely chopped dill

sea salt and freshly ground pepper

½ tablespoon olive oil

1 teaspoon butter

100 g smoked salmon, finely chopped, or 1 x 200 g can pink salmon, drained

1 x 200 g bag baby spinach leaves

Preheat your grill to high. Whisk the eggs, egg whites and yoghurt with half the grated parmesan. Add the dill and season with salt and pepper.

Heat the oil and butter in a non-stick, ovenproof frying pan over a low–medium heat. Pour in the egg mixture and let it settle. Sprinkle the smoked salmon evenly over the surface, followed by the spinach leaves. Cook over a low heat for 8–10 minutes, or until set.

Sprinkle the rest of the parmesan over the top and place under the hot grill until it bubbles. Cut the frittata into wedges and serve hot or cold.

SERVES 2

Goat's cheese and asparagus frittata

A little goat's cheese transforms this frittata. You could also make it in the morning and serve it as a cold lunch. Just don't eat the whole thing yourself!

3 eggs

2 egg whites

sea salt and freshly ground pepper

½ tablespoon extra-virgin olive oil

1 teaspoon butter

5 thin spears asparagus, woody ends trimmed

60 g marinated goat's cheese cheese, broken into small pieces

¼ cup grated parmesan cheese

Preheat your grill to high. Whisk the eggs and egg whites and season with salt and pepper.

Heat the oil and butter in a non-stick, ovenproof frying pan over a medium heat. Pour in the egg mixture and let it settle for 1–2 minutes. Arrange the asparagus spears over the surface and dot with pieces of goat's cheese. Cook for a further 4–5 minutes, or until almost set.

Sprinkle the parmesan over the top and place under the hot grill for 2–3 minutes, or until golden. Cut the frittata into wedges and serve hot or cold.

SERVES 2

`But I can't cook.´

What are you, a baby?

Of course you can.

Get a frying pan, turn on the heat,
sprinkle some sea salt and pepper
on a steak, add some olive oil, cook
the steak.

Look, you cooked.

Asparagus with poached egg and parmesan

....

This dish is often served as starter, but it's such a seriously great combination why not try it for breakfast one day?

8 spears asparagus, woody ends trimmed

2 eggs

parmesan cheese

drizzle of extra-virgin olive oil

splash of lemon juice

sea salt and freshly ground pepper

Fill a saucepan a quarter full with water, add a pinch of sea salt and bring to the boil. Add the asparagus and cook for around 3 minutes, or until the asparagus is just tender. Drain the asparagus and refresh under cold water for a few seconds. Drain again.

Meanwhile, poach the eggs to your liking.

Divide the asparagus spears between 2 plates, scatter a few shavings of parmesan on top and drizzle with a little olive oil and lemon juice. Top with a poached egg and season with salt and pepper.

SERVES 2

Spinachkopita

With respect to my Greek friends, this is spanakopita without the boombah (i.e. all the pastry and butter). I love the combination of spinach, feta and spring onion and it's certainly much more flavoursome than a regular spinach pie. Frozen spinach is perfect for this dish – just make sure you squeeze out all the water. The best thing of all is that you just bung all the ingredients into one bowl, give them a quick mix, then bake!

1 x 250 g packet frozen spinach, thawed and well drained

2 eggs, beaten

100 g Greek feta cheese, crumbled

1 tablespoon Greek yoghurt

1 tablespoon olive oil

6 spring onions, chopped

large handful flat-leaf parsley leaves, chopped

juice of ½ lemon

sea salt and freshly ground pepper

¼ cup grated parmesan cheese

Preheat the oven to 180°C.

Combine all the ingredients, except for the parmesan, in a large mixing bowl. Stir together until evenly combined then tip into a small ovenproof dish (Pyrex is ideal). Smooth the surface with a knife then sprinkle on the parmesan cheese. Bake for 45–50 minutes, or until the surface is golden brown and bubbling.

Remove the spinachkopita from the oven and leave to cool before cutting into wedges.

SERVES 4

Porridge with blueberries

Who knew there was such a palaver about oats? Porridge purists will scoff at my use of 'instant' porridge that you cook in the microwave for breakfast. But here's the news: these oats basically have the same nutritional value as your 'I-got-up-at-5 am-and-now-I'm-in-front-of-a-stove-stirring-a-pot-for-hours' oats. If you have the time to do that, then go right ahead. But for the rest of us, here's the fast track.

No, you *cannot* add honey.

½ cup instant oats
½ cup blueberries
½ cup skim or low-fat milk

Cook the porridge in a microwave-safe container according to the instructions on the box. When there is 1 minute of cooking time to go, add the blueberries. Cook for the final minute then remove from the microwave and leave to sit for 1 minute. Stir in the cold milk and enjoy. But be careful – the blueberries are hot!

SERVES 1

Feta, watermelon, red onion and black olives

Clearly I'm a girl with savoury tastes as this is my kind of breakfast. I remember this dish from a holiday in Turkey. Watermelon with feta was always served at the breakfast buffet and I adored it. Sure, it works much better in summer – but I think it's a real winner any time you can get watermelon.

¼ watermelon, deseeded and cut into chunks
100 g Greek feta cheese
½ red onion, finely sliced
handful of small black olives
drizzle of extra-virgin olive oil
splash of lemon juice

Arrange the watermelon, feta, onion and olives on a plate. Drizzle with a little olive oil and lemon juice and serve.

SERVES 1

Breakfast 'mess'

Here is my take on the classic Eton Mess. You know, the schoolboy 'rah rah' dessert that always looks so pretty? Gotta love that name … gotta hate the calories from all the cream, sugar and meringue. So, if you need a fruity kick at breakfast, here's my version. The crunchy part comes from almonds: just wrap them in a tea towel and smash them with a rolling pin. There you go – a quick morning workout!

2 tablespoons Greek yoghurt
50 g raspberries
50 g strawberries
6–8 blanched almonds, smashed coarsely

Mix the yoghurt with the berries and spoon into a small glass bowl or brandy balloon. Sprinkle with the smashed almonds and serve immediately.

SERVES 1

Salads, Soups & Starters

When you're trying to change the way you eat, some meals – such as lunch – can be a bit of a pain at first. It's especially tricky if you work away from home as the outside food world is simply not set up to help. So from now on, it's goodbye to boombah, store-bought buttery pies, creamy pastas and salty noodles, and hello to tasty, filling salads and soups you'll love. The soups in particular are ideal for lunch. You can make them the night before and take them with you to work in a flask.

With these lunches, you'll find that you have much more energy because you're not digesting all those useless carbohydrates that sit so heavily in your belly. And I guarantee you won't fall into that mid-afternoon 'nanna nap' slump.

All the dishes in this chapter are very easy to prepare and, as well as making wonderful light lunches, would also do double-duty as a starter for your next glamorous dinner party!

Roasted beetroot soup with a dollop of yoghurt

This soup looks so beautiful – all jewelled crimson with a splash of white – and the flavour is really enhanced by roasting the beetroot. It makes a great winter soup when there are fewer vegetables around to choose from. Serve as a light lunch or as a starter, and remember you don't need a whopping big serve!

3 large beetroots, heads and tails trimmed

2 tablespoons extra-virgin olive oil

sea salt and freshly ground pepper

1 large leek, washed and sliced into rings

1 litre salt-reduced chicken stock

1 tablespoon Greek yoghurt

freshly snipped chives

Preheat the oven to 180°C. Arrange the beetroots on an oven tray. Drizzle with 1 tablespoon of the olive oil and season with salt and pepper. Roast for 1½ hours or until tender. When cool enough to handle, rub off and discard the skins and chop the beetroot into chunks. It's a good idea to wear 'sandwich' gloves so your hands don't stain.

Heat the rest of the olive oil in a large saucepan over a low–medium heat. Add the leek and sauté gently until soft and translucent, being careful not to brown it. Add the chopped beetroot and the chicken stock, bring to the boil then lower the heat and simmer for 10 minutes.

Remove from the heat and allow to cool a little before blending to a smooth purée. If the soup is too much like beetroot dip, add a little more stock or water until you are happy with the consistency.

Reheat if necessary and season with salt and pepper. Ladle into warmed bowls and serve topped with a dollop of yoghurt and a sprinkling of chives.

SERVES 4

Prosciutto, melon and goat's cheese salad

I absolutely love prosciutto. It's reasonably priced and the thinner the slice, the better the taste (at least that's what I reckon). I think it's an acceptable treat and this traditional Italian starter is transformed with just a touch of insanely delicious marinated goat's cheese.

3 thin slices prosciutto

¼ cantaloupe (rockmelon), thinly sliced

30 g marinated goat's cheese

Arrange the prosciutto and the melon on a plate. Crumble on the goat's cheese and drizzle everything with a teaspoon of the oil from the goat's cheese jar. Serve immediately.

SERVES 1

Smoked salmon, onion and horseradish cream

One of my favourite restaurants in Melbourne is a French restaurant called France Soir, and I usually have smoked salmon as a starter. Here's my version of their elegant dish. (You are not required to speak French when you eat it.)

3 slices smoked salmon

¼ red onion, finely sliced into rings

2 teaspoons horseradish cream

1 tablespoon Greek yoghurt

freshly ground pepper

lemon wedge

Arrange the smoked salmon slices on a small plate and scatter the onion rings on top. Mix the horseradish and yoghurt together and drizzle in lines over the salmon and on the plate. Season with pepper and serve with a lemon wedge.

SERVES 1

Ladies' luncheon chicken salad

I have no idea why I call this dish 'ladies' luncheon'.
(It drives my dad mad.) I guess it just reminds me of
something that two ladies might eat as they catch up
over a light lunch. However, I do believe it is acceptable
for men to eat this salad too.

**200 g barbecued chicken,
finely shredded, skin removed**

**1 stick celery, finely sliced on
the diagonal**

**2 spring onions, finely sliced
on the diagonal**

**handful of raw snow peas,
finely sliced on the diagonal**

¼ cup walnut halves

salt and freshly ground pepper

freshly snipped chives

DRESSING

1 tablespoon mayonnaise

1 tablespoon Greek yoghurt

1 teaspoon soy sauce

juice of ½ lime

To make the dressing, combine the
mayonnaise, yoghurt, soy sauce and lime
juice in a small bowl.

In another bowl, combine the shredded
chicken, celery, spring onions, snow peas
and walnuts. Add the dressing and toss
together gently. Season with salt and pepper
and divide between 2 bread and butter
plates. Sprinkle with chives and serve.

SERVES 2

Creamy broccoli and leek soup

I think I could eat soup for lunch every day – I don't have to wait for winter. The creaminess in this recipe comes from the smooth taste of the vegies and a dollop of yoghurt instead of cream. The mustard adds a surprising lift.

2 tablespoons extra-virgin olive oil

2 cloves garlic, roughly chopped

375 g broccoli florets (or you could use cauliflower)

1 leek, cleaned and finely chopped

1 tablespoon wholegrain mustard

1 litre salt-reduced chicken stock

2 tablespoons oregano leaves

1 tablespoon Greek yoghurt

sea salt and freshly ground pepper

4 basil leaves

Heat the olive oil in a large saucepan over a medium heat. Add the garlic, broccoli, leek and mustard and sauté for about 5 minutes, stirring often. Add the stock and oregano and bring to the boil. Lower the heat and simmer, covered, for about 20 minutes.

Remove from the heat and allow to cool a little before blending to a smooth purée. Add the yoghurt and season to taste with salt and pepper. When ready to serve, reheat if necessary and ladle into warmed bowls. Garnish with a basil leaf.

SERVES 4

We all need food we can
look forward to.

Rare roast beef rolls
with vegies

There's no need to cook a piece of beef yourself as most delicatessens can carve a few slices for you (although it's a great way to use up any leftovers). Ask for the slices to be nice and thin.

1 tablespoon Greek yoghurt

½ tablespoon mayonnaise

thin scraping of hot English or French mustard

2 thin slices rare roast beef

2 spring onions, finely shredded

1 stick celery, cut into julienne strips

½ carrot, cut into julienne strips

¼ continental cucumber, cut into julienne strips

salt and freshly ground pepper

Mix the yoghurt, mayonnaise and mustard and spread a thin layer on each slice of roast beef. Arrange the vegetables in an even line down the centre of the beef slices, season with salt and pepper and roll them up like sushi.

SERVES 1

Asian-style crab omelette

This is a fabulous Sunday brunch or starter. The Asian flavours make it tasty and light and a little bit posh. A side salad of lettuce leaves dressed with a little sesame oil and lemon juice works well as an accompaniment.

2 eggs

1 egg white

1 x 170 g can crab meat, drained

2 spring onions, finely sliced (reserve the green tops)

2 teaspoons sesame oil

2 teaspoons light soy sauce

2 teaspoons peanut oil

½ cup bean sprouts

Preheat your grill to high. In a large mixing bowl, whisk the eggs and egg white together lightly. Add the crab, spring onions, sesame oil and soy sauce.

Heat a small, non-stick, ovenproof frying pan over a high heat. Pour in the peanut oil and, when it sizzles, lower the heat and add the egg mixture. Cook for 2 minutes, stirring occasionally. Cook for a further 3 minutes, or until the omelette is nearly set. Place under the grill until it turns golden.

To serve, fold omelette and sprinkle with the bean sprouts and green spring onion tops.

SERVES 2

Barbecued chook
with shredded Asian coleslaw

Go to your supermarket, buy a barbecued chook and a bag of mixed coleslaw (not drenched in a creamy dressing please) and presto! You have an easy and satisfying meal that won't leave you wanting to raid the cookie jar.

¼ **barbecued chicken**

1 **teaspoon sesame oil**

1 **tablespoon extra-virgin olive oil**

1 **teaspoon light soy sauce**

squeeze of lemon juice

1 x 100 g **bag coleslaw, without dressing**

Pull one of the breasts off the chicken and use your fingers to shred the meat (I also include the skin, but if you're being tough, discard the skin). Keep the rest of the chicken in the fridge for another meal.

Combine the oils, soy sauce and lemon juice to make a dressing.

Tip the coleslaw into a bowl, top with the shredded chicken, and drizzle the dressing over the lot. Toss and serve.

SERVES 1

Cauliflower soup with prawns and chilli oil

This is a creamy, smooth winter soup with a chilli oil kick and a fancy prawn bonus. It looks classy and tastes delicious.

500 ml salt-reduced chicken stock

250 ml skim milk

250 ml water

1 cauliflower, chopped into florets

1 clove garlic, crushed

sea salt and freshly ground pepper

1 teaspoon extra-virgin olive oil

4 large green prawns, cleaned, shelled, deveined, with tails intact

chilli oil

Combine the stock, skim milk and water in a large saucepan. Bring to the boil and add the cauliflower florets and garlic. Lower the heat to a simmer and cook for about 8 minutes, or until the cauliflower is just tender.

Transfer the cooked cauliflower to a blender or food processor and reserve the cooking liquid in another big bowl. Whiz the cauliflower to a purée, adding some of the liquid to help make a smooth consistency. Tip back into the saucepan and heat gently. Keep adding stock, a little at a time, until you are happy with the consistency. Season to taste with salt and pepper and keep on a low simmer.

Heat the olive oil in a small frying pan and sauté the prawns for about 2 minutes, or until they turn a reddish colour. Season with a little salt and pepper. Ladle the soup into bowls and top with a prawn. Drizzle with a little chilli oil and serve immediately.

SERVES 4

Roasted red capsicum soup

It may just be me who's noticed, but there seems to be a bit of a carry-on about taking the skin off capsicums. I reckon that charring them on a stove hob wreaks havoc with your element, while placing the blackened capsicums in a plastic bag, waiting for them to cool and then peeling them seems a bit fiddly and time-consuming. It's much easier just to roast them and then peel the skin off when they're cool.

3 large red capsicums

2 cloves garlic, unpeeled

3 large ripe tomatoes

1 tablespoon extra-virgin olive oil

500 ml salt-reduced vegetable stock

sea salt and freshly ground pepper

2 teaspoons Greek yoghurt (optional)

Preheat the oven to 170°C. Arrange the capsicums, garlic and tomatoes on an oven tray. Drizzle with the olive oil and roast for about 40 minutes. Remove from the oven and leave to cool. Peel the capsicums and tomatoes and discard the skins and seeds of both. Peel the garlic and discard the skin. Chop everything roughly then blend in a food processor until smooth.

Heat the vegetable stock in a large saucepan until it begins to simmer. Add the purée gradually, stirring until the consistency is to your liking. Add salt and pepper to taste and simmer gently for a few minutes. Ladle the soup into warmed bowls and top with a dollop of yoghurt, if using. Serve with a Parmesan Crisp (page 69) if you're in a fancy mood.

SERVES 4

Prawns on a plate

I've spoken with many chefs who say they can't take prawn cocktail off their menus, and I totally get it. The combination of chilled, plump prawns with daggy but delicious Marie Rose sauce is a winner. I just don't dig the retro prawns-in-a-glass look, so forgive me as I present 'prawns on a plate'.

By the way, this is the *only* time I let you get away with serving tomato sauce.

10 green prawns, cleaned, shelled, deveined, with tails intact

1 tablespoon mayonnaise

1 tablespoon Greek yoghurt

1 teaspoon tomato sauce

1 teaspoon Worcestershire sauce (or a pinch of dried chilli flakes)

squeeze of lemon juice

good dash of Tabasco

salt and freshly ground pepper

¼ iceberg lettuce, shredded

6 small cherry tomatoes, quartered

½ avocado, cut into small cubes

lemon wedges

Drop the prawns into a large saucepan of salted, boiling water. Remove with a slotted spoon as they rise to the surface and transfer to a bowl of chilled water.

Combine the mayonnaise, yoghurt, ketchup, Worcestershire sauce, lemon juice and Tabasco in a small bowl and whisk together to make a sauce. Season with salt and pepper and set aside.

Form a row of shredded lettuce across the centre of 2 plates. Arrange the tomatoes and avocado on top of the lettuce, followed by the prawns. Finish with a drizzle of sauce across each dish and serve with wedges of lemon on the side.

SERVES 2

It's a very impressive look when you just grab a handful of herbs from your own garden and throw them into your dish!

Oysters Kilpatrick

You just can't beat the combination of creamy oyster, salty bacon and Worcestershire sauce. Yum.

(You do know Worcestershire is made from anchovies, don't you?)

8 freshly shucked oysters, in their shells

Worcestershire sauce

2 rashers bacon, finely chopped

freshly ground pepper

flat-leaf parsley leaves, chopped

Preheat your grill to high. Arrange the oysters on an oven tray. Add a splash of Worcestershire sauce to each oyster and top with bacon. Place under the grill until the bacon just starts to get crisp and brown at the edges. Serve immediately with a sprinkle of pepper and parsley.

SERVES 2

Fennel, orange and parsley salad

This has crunch, tang and colour – everything you're after in a salad. The aniseedy fennel adds a point of difference.

1 fennel bulb, top trimmed and outer layers removed

1 orange, peeled and pith removed, thinly sliced

10 black olives

1 cup flat-leaf parsley leaves

1 tablespoon extra-virgin olive oil

juice of 1 lemon

salt and freshly ground pepper

Cut the fennel crosswise into thin slices. Place in a bowl with the orange slices, olives and parsley, and drizzle with the oil and lemon juice. Toss gently and season with salt and pepper. Serve immediately.

SERVES 2

Calamari with rocket, chilli, sesame seeds and garlic

I don't cook calamari all that often because, to be honest, it's not that easy to make it nice and tender without boombah-crumbing-and-frying it. But I love the toasty taste of the sesame seeds in this salad. I'm not very keen on the look of calamari rings, so I suggest cutting the tube into small squares, which miraculously curl up and become cool mini tubes.

1 calamari tube, cleaned

sea salt and freshly ground pepper

200 g rocket leaves

1 tablespoon vegetable oil

1 teaspoon sesame oil

2 small red chillies, finely chopped

2 cloves garlic, finely chopped

juice of 1 lemon

1 teaspoon sesame seeds, lightly toasted

lemon wedges

To prepare the calamari, cut down one side of the tube and open it out flat to form a rectangle. Use a sharp knife to lightly score the inside surface of the calamari with a cross-hatch pattern. Cut into small rectangles and season with salt and pepper.

Arrange the rocket on a serving platter.

Heat the two oils in a large frying pan and fry the chilli and garlic for about 30 seconds. Add the calamari and stir-fry over a high heat until it starts to curl up and colour slightly.

Tip the calamari onto the rocket leaves (make sure you include all the bits of chilli and garlic), squeeze on the lemon juice, sprinkle with sesame seeds and serve with lemon wedges on the side.

SERVES 2

Scallops with cauliflower purée and apple

．．．．．．．．．．．．．．．．．

Scallops sound very fancy, but they're not expensive and they're so quick to cook. Combining them with cauliflower purée sounds crazy, but it works – especially when you throw in some peppery watercress and fresh, tangy apple. Make sure you've got hot plates for serving.

6 fresh scallops (I prefer the large white ones without roe)

½ cauliflower, cut into florets

½ cup water

1 tablespoon Greek yoghurt

salt and freshly ground pepper

½ tablespoon extra-virgin olive oil

½ teaspoon butter

1 teaspoon good-quality curry powder

½ Granny Smith apple, peeled and cut into matchsticks

handful of watercress leaves

If your scallops still have their roe attached, remove it and discard. Slice each scallop in half crosswise, so you have 16 discs in total. Cover and refrigerate until ready to serve.

Place the cauliflower florets and water in a microwave-safe container with a lid. Microwave on full power for 6–7 minutes. Tip into a food processor and add the yoghurt, salt and pepper and whiz to a smooth purée. Set aside and keep warm.

Heat the olive oil and butter in a heavy-based frying pan over a high heat. Dust the scallops with the curry powder then add to the pan and fry for 1 minute. Turn and fry for another minute, until they are just golden.

Smear a spoonful of the cauliflower purée onto 2 warmed plates, then arrange the scallops on top. Arrange the apple sticks and watercress and serve straight away.

SERVES 2

Let's Party

Ever since I saw Cher serving her children hors d'oeuvres for dinner in the movie *Mermaids*, I've adored the idea of living on trays of canapés myself! Seriously, if you're having a 'do', don't get stressed or feel obliged to serve your friends stodgy fried or boombah food.

Get excited! Celebrate and share your new healthy food discoveries! Here are some canapés that you could also transform into starters; they are delicious and easy and look impressive.

Parmesan crisps

You will be in love with me after you try these crisps. They take so little time to make and are a brilliant cracker substitute. Following this recipe are some delicious toppings.

Oh, and it's just a suggestion, but don't eat the whole plate yourself. Try to leave some for your guests.

1 x 250 g packet shredded parmesan cheese (or freshly grated parmesan)

Preheat the oven to 200°C. Line a baking tray with baking paper.

Place teaspoonfuls of grated parmesan on the baking tray, leaving about 3 cm between them to allow for spreading. Bake for 7–10 minutes until bubbling and golden – not brown. Remove from the oven and carefully lift the baking paper – crisps and all – off the tray.

Use a wide spatula to lift the crisps onto a wire rack to cool – you'll find that they crisp up as they cool down. The parmesan crisps will stay fresh for up to 3 days if wrapped in baking paper and stored in an airtight container.

MAKES AROUND 16

Chilli crab

1 x 170 g can crab meat

1 small red chilli, finely chopped (deseeded if you don't want it too hot)

1 tablespoon mayonnaise

1 tablespoon Greek yoghurt

zest of ½ lemon

sea salt and freshly ground pepper

sprigs of dill

Combine all the ingredients, except for the dill, in a mixing bowl. Stir together gently but evenly. Place small dollops on top of the Parmesan Crisps and garnish with a sprig of dill.

MAKES ENOUGH TO TOP AROUND 16 PARMESAN CRISPS

Roast beef and Dijonnaise

2–3 large slices rare roast beef

1 tablespoon Dijon mustard

1 tablespoon mayonnaise

1 tablespoon Greek yoghurt

sea salt and freshly ground pepper

Cut each slice of beef into pieces around the same size as the Parmesan Crisps. Combine the mustard, mayonnaise and yoghurt in a small bowl. Place a piece of beef on each crisp, sprinkle with salt and pepper and top with a dollop of the mustard mayo.

MAKES ENOUGH TO TOP AROUND 16 PARMESAN CRISPS

Smoked salmon and crème fraîche

100 g smoked salmon, cut into
bite-sized pieces

zest of ½ lemon

100 g crème fraîche

sprigs of dill

Place a piece of salmon on each Parmesan
Crisp. Mix the lemon zest into the crème
fraîche and carefully place ½ teaspoon
dollops on top of the salmon. Garnish
with dill and serve straight away.

MAKES ENOUGH TO TOP AROUND
16 PARMESAN CRISPS

Italian spinach

2 big handfuls of baby spinach
leaves, well washed

1 tablespoon extra-virgin
olive oil

1 clove garlic, finely chopped

salt and freshly ground pepper

parmesan cheese shavings

Blanch the spinach in a large saucepan
of boiling water for 1 minute, then drain
thoroughly and squeeze out as much excess
water as you can.

Heat the oil in a frying pan over a low–
medium heat. Add the garlic and sauté
gently for about 1 minute, taking care not
to let it brown. Add the spinach, stir until
heated through and until any moisture has
evaporated. Remove the pan from the heat
and season to taste with salt and pepper.
Leave to cool a little, then chop the spinach
neatly. Top each Parmesan Crisp with
a spoonful of spinach and finish with a
parmesan shaving.

MAKES ENOUGH TO TOP AROUND
16 PARMESAN CRISPS

Prawns in snow peas

I know this is just peas and prawns, but they look great – all lime green and pink. The crunchy snow peas make delicious 'boat' containers for the prawn mixture. You could easily add a touch of chilli or cayenne pepper for a bit of extra zing. This is another dish that I've turned into an entrée on many occasions.

1 tablespoon mayonnaise

1 tablespoon Greek yoghurt

salt and freshly ground pepper

10 freshly cooked prawns, finely chopped

1 tablespoon freshly snipped chives

20 large snow peas

In a small bowl, combine the mayonnaise and yoghurt and season with salt and pepper. Add the chopped prawns and chives and stir well to combine.

Split each snow pea open to make a boat. Place a teaspoon of the prawn mixture inside each snow pea and serve.

MAKES 20

Tuna on cucumber with wasabi mayo and nori sprinkle

These look very 'zen' and are so easy to prepare. Buy best-quality sashimi tuna and cut it into small rectangles. Cut slices of cucumber into the same shape. Place the tuna on the cucumber and top with small dollops of mayonnaise flavoured with wasabi. Sprinkle with shredded nori and serve.

Olives with lemon and herbs

Place a small tub (about 225 g) of good-quality, large, unpitted green olives into a saucepan with 2 tablespoons of best extra-virgin olive oil, the zest of 1 lemon and a sprig each of thyme and rosemary. Heat gently for about 10 minutes for the flavours to infuse. Tip into an attractive bowl and serve. Remember to also offer a smaller side bowl for the stones!

SERVES 4–6

Cheese puffs

I used to have a bit of a penchant for cheesy gougères –
those golden balls of batter that take about a month to
walk off. So I set about trying to create that light, cheesy
taste without the calories and 'poof', here they are! They're
so moreish that they almost seem too good to be true, but
you do need to make sure they're eaten straight out of the
oven or they will start drooping and look a bit sad.

4 egg whites

**1 tablespoon grated tasty
cheddar cheese**

**1 tablespoon grated
parmesan cheese**

pinch of cayenne pepper

pinch of white pepper

pinch of sea salt

Preheat the oven to 200ºC. Line a baking
tray with baking paper.

Whisk the egg whites to form soft peaks.
Gently fold in the two cheeses, the cayenne
and white pepper and salt.

Place neat rounded spoonfuls of the mixture
on the baking tray, leaving about 3 cm
between them to allow for spreading. Bake
for 8–10 minutes, or until golden brown.
Serve immediately.

MAKES 16-20

'Here, have a piece of bread. You have to eat bread.'

'Aren't you eating pasta?'

'What? No rice? Well, that's just weird.'

Be firm. Stick to your guns.

Tuna 'sushi' rolls

I have mixed feelings about the world of sushi. Although I'm happy that people choose sushi rolls over, say, fried chicken, I honestly don't think they realise how many calories there are in one of those tubes of rice. It's sweetened, gluggy rice too, which makes the dish stodgy. Trust me, once the rice is gone it tastes heaps better.

1 sheet nori

1 x 120 g can tuna in springwater or 100 g sashimi grade tuna

2 teaspoons mayonnaise

¼ teaspoon wasabi

5 cm piece of cucumber, deseeded and cut lengthwise into strips

¼ avocado, cut lengthwise into strips

light soy sauce for dipping

Use scissors to cut the nori sheet in half to form 2 rectangles.

Mix the canned tuna with the mayonnaise and wasabi and spoon it along the centre of each piece of nori. If using fresh tuna, slice it very thinly and layer it over the nori. Top with cucumber and avocado strips. Roll up each nori sheet to form a sushi roll. Serve with light soy sauce for dipping.

SERVES 1

What's for Dinner?

By the end of the day I don't have the time or energy to fiddle about with dinner, so here are some recipes for fast, flashy meals. I've tried to make them as satisfying, tasty and low in calories as possible and, for me, that means leaving out the boombah bits, such as white rice, pasta and mashed potato.

I promise that you'll enjoy this
healthy way of eating without
feeling as if you're missing out
– and even better, you'll go to bed
without that bloated feeling.
All these recipes have evolved after
lots of experimenting in my own
kitchen at home.

Tasty pepper steak with hot horseradish cream

....

If we have steak for dinner I often choose a porterhouse for flavour. However feel free to choose your favourite cut – a juicy T-bone can work just as well. Supermarkets have amazingly good quality meat available these days, and I've also been known to grab a few steaks from the local 7-Eleven to serve as a quick meal for unexpected friends who drop by. (Who am I kidding? We have no unexpected friends who want to call into our madhouse … I just wanted to sound sociable.)

2 x 130 g beef porterhouse or scotch steaks

extra-virgin olive oil

sea salt and freshly ground pepper

HOT HORSERADISH CREAM

1 tablespoon horseradish cream*

1 tablespoon Greek yoghurt

1 teaspoon hot English mustard

* Keep a lookout for fresh horseradish when it comes into season as it is even better than the ready-prepared version. Simply grate a teaspoon of the root and mix with a few drops of white wine vinegar before preparing as described in the method above.

To make the hot horseradish cream, mix the ingredients thoroughly and chill.

Preheat the oven to 210°C. Heat an ovenproof frying pan over a high heat until it is really, really hot.

Rub the steaks all over with a little olive oil then season generously with salt and pepper. Place the steaks in the very hot frying pan and cook for 3 minutes on one side. Turn over and cook on the other side for 2 minutes. Transfer the pan to the oven and cook a further 6 minutes, which will cook the steaks pink (medium–rare). Remember that the handle of the pan will be hot, so use 2 oven mitts or tea towels when removing it from the oven.

Remove the steaks from the pan and transfer to a warm plate. Cover with aluminium foil and leave to rest for 4–5 minutes. Pour any juices back into the pan and return it to the stove top. Heat gently, scraping up any pepper and other yummy bits stuck to the bottom. Pour over the steaks and serve with hot horseradish cream.

SERVES 2

Chilli, lime and garlic beef

This dish came about from an experimental 'what-have-I-got-in-the-fridge' moment. It's actually quite tricky to cook a good stir-fry. You should do it in stages and never overcrowd the wok or frying pan or the ingredients will stew instead of fry. Don't overcook the vegies either – they should still have some crunch.

½ tablespoon peanut oil

2 cloves garlic, finely chopped

1 small knob of ginger, peeled and finely chopped

2 small red chillies, finely chopped

240 g beef scotch fillet, quite thinly sliced

1 teaspoon sesame oil

1 onion, finely sliced

½ green capsicum, chopped

3 spears asparagus, woody ends trimmed, chopped

3 spring onions, chopped

2 kaffir lime leaves, very finely sliced

Heat the peanut oil in a wok or frying pan over a high heat. Add the garlic, ginger and chilli and stir-fry for about 30 seconds. Add the beef and stir-fry for 4 minutes. Keep the ingredients moving to stop the garlic and chilli burning. Remove everything from the pan and add the sesame oil.

Still over a high heat, add the onion and capsicum and stir-fry for about a minute. Add the asparagus and spring onions and cook for a further minute. Finally, add the kaffir lime leaves and the beef and stir briefly just to warm the beef. Divide between 2 warmed bowls and serve straight away.

SERVES 2

Chilli tuna steaks
with wasabi coleslaw

This is another firm favourite standby meal. Use only the freshest tuna and make sure it is a lovely ruby colour with no fishy smell. You can leave out the chilli flakes if you don't like spicy food. The coleslaw also goes brilliantly with lamb chops or chicken.

2 x 140 g tuna steaks

2 teaspoons extra-virgin olive oil

pinch of dried chilli flakes

sea salt and freshly ground pepper

lime wedges

coriander leaves

WASABI COLESLAW

¼ red cabbage, finely sliced

¼ white cabbage, finely sliced

2 spring onions, finely sliced on the diagonal

handful of snow peas, finely sliced on the diagonal

1 tablespoon mayonnaise

1 tablespoon Greek yoghurt

wasabi paste to taste

To make the coleslaw, combine the cabbage, spring onions and snow peas in a mixing bowl.

In a smaller bowl mix the mayonnaise and yoghurt to make a creamy dressing, then add as much or as little wasabi as you like. I find it best to start with a small squeeze and increase to taste. Add the dressing to the coleslaw ingredients and toss to combine thoroughly. Cover and refrigerate until ready to serve.

To prepare the tuna steaks, rub them all over with a little olive oil then sprinkle with a good pinch of dried chilli flakes and season generously with salt and pepper.

Heat a non-stick frying pan over a high heat. Place the tuna in the pan then lower the heat to medium–high. Cook for around 4 minutes then turn and cook for 2 minutes on the other side. This will cook the tuna medium–rare. Cook for 6 minutes on one side and 3 minutes on the other if you prefer it well-done.

Serve the tuna steaks with coleslaw on top, lime wedges on the side and scattered with coriander leaves.

SERVES 2

Moroccan chicken tagine

I'm a bit of a newcomer to Moroccan flavours but I'm a convert. Chermoula is a spice paste that includes cumin, paprika, turmeric, cayenne pepper, garlic, onion and coriander. You can buy it from some supermarkets these days, but if you're struggling, specialty food stores or delicatessens will stock it – just check that the sugar content is low.

4 small skinless chicken fillets

2 tablespoons chermoula paste

juice of 1 lemon

1 tablespoon extra-virgin olive oil

1 onion, thinly sliced

2 cloves garlic, thinly sliced

1 small knob of ginger, peeled and finely grated

½ lemon, finely sliced

½ cup pitted green olives

1 cinnamon stick

500 ml salt-reduced chicken stock

coriander leaves

Place the chicken fillets in a zip-lock bag with the chermoula paste and lemon juice and squeeze and squish it all around so the chicken is evenly coated. Refrigerate for 10–15 minutes for the flavours to infuse.

Heat the oil in a large, heavy-based casserole dish or tagine and fry the onion, garlic and ginger for around 2 minutes, taking care not to burn them. Add the chicken to the pan and cook on a medium–high heat for 2–3 minutes, or until the chicken turns golden. Add the lemon slices, olives, cinnamon stick and stock and bring to the boil. Once it starts to bubble, lower the heat and simmer gently for 1 hour with the lid on.

When ready to serve, take out the cinnamon stick and divide the tagine between 4 warmed plates. Sprinkle with coriander leaves and serve with Cauliflower 'Rice' (page 151).

SERVES 4

Herb and peppered eye fillet beef with celeriac and horseradish mash

Celeriac is my new favourite vegetable, especially when it's made into mash. It's only available in winter in Australia and is very versatile. If you can't find celeriac, you could serve the beef with pumpkin or sweet potato mash.

1 x 1 kg whole beef eye fillet

1 tablespoon extra-virgin olive oil

1 tablespoon sea salt

1 tablespoon freshly ground black pepper

½ cup rosemary leaves, chopped

½ cup thyme leaves, chopped

½ cup flat-leaf parsley leaves, chopped

½ cup basil leaves, chopped

small handful of celery leaves

CELERIAC AND HORSERADISH MASH

1 celeriac root, peeled and chopped into chunks

1 teaspoon salt

1 tablespoon yoghurt

1 tablespoon horseradish cream

salt and freshly ground pepper

Preheat the oven to 220°C.

To cook the beef, rub it all over with olive oil and season with salt and pepper. Mix all the herbs (except for the celery leaves), then sprinkle them on a chopping board. Roll the beef around in the mixture until evenly coated. Place on an oven tray and roast for 20–25 minutes. Remove from the oven and transfer the beef to a warm plate. Cover with aluminium foil and leave to rest for 10 minutes before carving into slices.

To make the mash, place the celeriac in a large saucepan, cover with water, add the salt and bring to the boil. Lower the heat and simmer for about 15 minutes, or until the celeriac is tender. Drain well, then tip into a large mixing bowl with the yoghurt, horseradish, salt and pepper and mash until smooth. Alternatively, whiz to a purée with a hand-blender. Keep warm until ready to serve.

To serve, place a spoonful of celeriac mash on each plate and arrange slices of beef on top. Sprinkle with celery leaves and serve straight away.

SERVES 4

Jane Kennedy

Swordfish with capsicum relish

Capers are the key to this dish as they add an unexpected salty flavour. And by cooking the fish in a low oven (as opposed to pan- or deep-frying), it retains its moisture and is a low-calorie winner. You could easily use tuna steaks instead of swordfish, if you prefer.

2 small swordfish steaks

1 tablespoon capers (I love the salted ones)

handful of flat-leaf parsley leaves, chopped

zest and juice of 1 lemon

salt and freshly ground pepper

2 tablespoons extra-virgin olive oil

CAPSICUM RELISH

1 ½ tablespoons extra-virgin olive oil

2 red capsicums, seeds and membranes removed, chopped

2 cloves garlic, chopped

2 large ripe tomatoes, peeled and chopped

sea salt and freshly ground pepper

To make the capsicum relish, heat the oil in a saucepan over a low–medium heat. Add all the remaining ingredients and bring to the boil, stirring well. Lower the heat and simmer gently, covered, for 25–30 minutes, or until all the ingredients are tender. Check and stir well every 10 minutes or so. Serve warm or cold.

Preheat the oven to 150°C. Place the swordfish steaks in an ovenproof dish.

In a small bowl, combine the capers, parsley, lemon zest, salt and pepper and mix well. Spoon onto each piece of fish then drizzle with olive oil and the lemon juice. Bake for 20–25 minutes then serve with the capsicum relish.

SERVES 2

Chilli, lemon, lime and coconut chicken

Plain chicken fillets are boring, so this is my attempt at zinging up the flavour without hours of marinating. Just adding a very small amount of light coconut milk transforms this dish. I made it the other night after buying all the ingredients from my local 7-Eleven at 8.30 pm. (Well, everything except the kaffir lime leaves, which I already had in my freezer.)

As a variation, I'll sometimes add some chopped bok choy or a few spears of asparagus to the pan with the coconut milk.

2 small skinless chicken breasts

2 small red chillies, chopped

2 cloves garlic, chopped

3 kaffir lime leaves, finely shredded

juice of 1 lemon

2 tablespoons extra-virgin olive oil

sea salt and freshly ground pepper

¼ cup light coconut milk

Wrap each chicken in clingfilm and use a rolling pin or heavy can to bash it flat. Don't be too vigorous – you don't want them to fall apart. Transfer to a zip-lock bag and add all the remaining ingredients, except for the coconut milk. Leave for 20 minutes for the flavours to infuse – although 10 will do.

Heat a non-stick frying pan over a high heat, then reduce the heat to medium. Use a pair of tongs to take the chicken out of the bag, making sure you leave the rest of the marinade ingredients behind. Fry the chicken breasts on one side until they just start to brown then turn and cook for another few minutes on the other side. Lower the heat and add the rest of the marinade ingredients to the pan with the coconut milk. Simmer for a further minute, then serve with a cos lettuce salad.

SERVES 2

What's for Dinner?

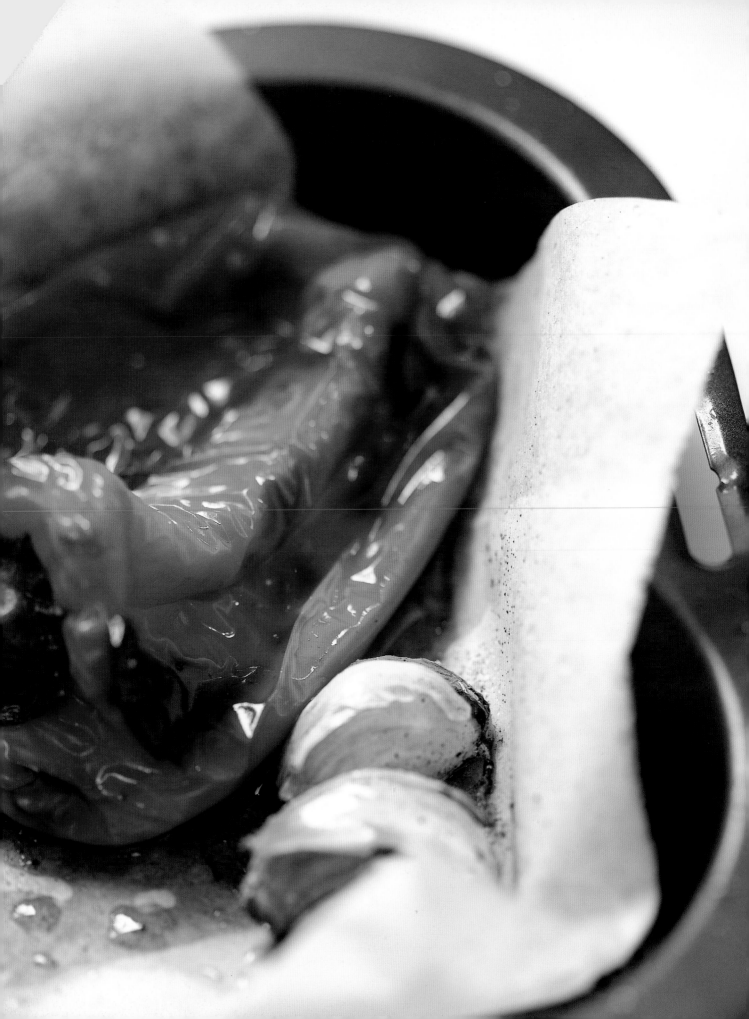

I just had to find a way to combine my love of food with my love of a particular dress size …

Bistecca con rucola

This sounds so much more exotic than saying 'steak and salad'. Lately, instead of buying a couple of steaks, I've taken to buying one large piece of fantastic quality beef – such as rib eye on the bone or a juicy T-bone. After cooking, I slice the meat and serve it on a bed of rocket on a platter in the middle of the table. It's so easy but looks so fancy.

It's important to take the meat out of your fridge at least 30 minutes before cooking to bring it to room temperature. It makes the meat tastier as the fibres will have had time to relax.

1 x 300 g piece beef rib eye

1 tablespoon extra-virgin olive oil

sea salt and freshly ground pepper

handful of rocket leaves

lemon wedges

Preheat the oven to 200°C. Heat a cast-iron frying pan until it's really, really hot.

Rub the beef all over with olive oil and season generously with salt and pepper.

Place the steak in the pan and cook for 3 minutes. Don't be tempted to turn it and have a look before the 3 minutes are up. Turn and cook on the other side for 1 minute then transfer to the oven and cook for around 8 minutes. This will give you a juicy, tender, rare steak. Cook for longer if you prefer your steak well-done. Remember that the handle of the pan will be hot, so use 2 oven mitts or tea towels when removing it from the oven.

Leave the beef to rest in a warm place for 5 minutes, then cut into nice thick slices on a diagonal. To serve, scatter the rocket leaves on a platter and arrange the slices of beef. Serve with lemon wedges.

SERVES 2

Thai fish cakes

Another great way to get a spicy Thai hit. These fish cakes make a great starter or can easily be turned into a canapé to serve with drinks if you make them bite-sized.

220 g ling or rockling fillets (or a similar firm white fish), cut into chunks

½ tablespoon fish sauce

½ tablespoon red curry paste

1 kaffir lime leaf, finely shredded

½ tablespoon coriander leaves

1 egg

½ teaspoon salt

10 green beans, thinly sliced

2 tablespoons sunflower or vegetable oil

extra coriander leaves

Place all the ingredients, except for the beans and oil, into a food processor and whiz to a smooth paste. Stir in the beans evenly. Roll the mixture into even-sized balls and flatten them to form cakes.

Heat the oil in a frying pan over a medium heat. Fry the fish cakes in batches for around 2½ minutes on each side, or until golden brown. Serve with a crisp green salad and scatter over coriander leaves.

SERVES 2

Lemony veal

....

For some reason we end up having this meal most Monday nights. Your butcher will flatten the veal into medium–thick scallopini for you if you ask sweetly. This dish can also be made with pork fillet.

2 x 120 g pieces good-quality veal, flattened

salt and freshly ground pepper

1 teaspoon butter

1 tablespoon extra-virgin olive oil

splash of white wine

juice of 1 lemon

Season the veal all over with salt and pepper.

Heat the butter and oil in a non-stick frying pan over a medium heat. Add the veal and fry for around 5 minutes. Turn and cook for a further 4 minutes, then pour in the white wine and let it sizzle. Add the lemon juice, and let it sizzle for a further minute. Remove the pan from the heat and serve the veal on warmed plates. Drizzle on the lemony sauce and serve with fresh salad or steamed broccolini.

SERVES 2

Jamie Oliver's seared beef fillet with chilli, ginger, radish and soy

This is one of my all-time favourite recipes, and it comes from Jamie's second cookbook, *The Return of the Naked Chef*. It's a ripping summer dish which looks impressive served on a platter. I like to eat this dish with chopsticks – somehow it just feels right!

½ tablespoon coriander seeds

½ tablespoon peppercorns

½ tablespoon sea salt

handful of rosemary leaves, finely chopped

1 x 220 g beef eye fillet

1 knob of ginger, peeled and cut into very fine batons

2 small red chillies, deseeded and finely sliced

8 small radishes, trimmed and thinly sliced

small handful of coriander leaves, chopped

2 teaspoons sesame oil

1 tablespoon light soy sauce or tamari

juice of 2 limes

Heat a heavy frying pan over a medium–high heat. Add the coriander seeds and move them around until the seeds start to pop and release their aroma. Tip into a mortar and pound to a powder with the peppercorns and salt, then mix in the rosemary. Sprinkle the mixture onto a chopping board and roll the beef around so it is evenly coated.

Heat the pan over a high heat then cook the beef for around 5 minutes, until brown and slightly crisp on all sides. Remove from the pan and leave to rest for 5 minutes.

When ready to serve, slice the beef into very thin slices and arrange on a platter. Sprinkle on the ginger, chilli, radish and coriander, then splash on the sesame oil and soy sauce. Lastly, squeeze on the lime juice, making sure all the meat is covered.

SERVES 2

Lamb cutlets with romesco sauce

Romesco sauce originates from Catalonia in Spain and it's the almonds that provide its unique taste. It also has plenty of kick! This is a different way to serve plain old lamb cutlets and also makes a cool dinner party main course. If there is any sauce left over it should keep for a couple of days in the fridge and you could serve it with fish or chicken.

6 Frenched lamb cutlets

1 tablespoon extra-virgin olive oil

sea salt and freshly ground pepper

10 small olives (your choice of colour)

ROMESCO SAUCE

1 red capsicum

2 cloves garlic, skin on

1 ½ tablespoons extra-virgin olive oil

¼ cup blanched almonds

1 small chilli, chopped

1 teaspoon red wine vinegar

juice of ½ lime

½ teaspoon smoked paprika

salt and freshly ground white pepper

To prepare the romesco sauce, first preheat the oven to 220°C. Arrange the capsicum and garlic cloves in an oven tray. Drizzle on ½ tablespoon of the oil and roast for 30–35 minutes. Remove from the oven and leave to cool. Peel the capsicums and garlic and discard the seeds and skins. Chop roughly and set aside.

Heat a heavy-based frying pan over a medium heat and fry the almonds, shaking continuously, until they are golden brown. Remove the nuts from the pan and leave to cool a little before grinding to a coarse powder (I use a clean coffee grinder to do this). Add the capsicum and garlic, together with the rest of the olive oil, the chilli, vinegar, lime juice, paprika, salt and pepper and process until smooth. If the sauce is too thick, add a little more olive oil.

When ready to cook the lamb cutlets, rub them all over with olive oil and season generously with salt and pepper. Heat a non-stick frying pan over a medium–high heat. Fry the cutlets on one side for around 2½ minutes, then turn and cook for a further 2 minutes. Remove from the pan and leave to rest for 2–3 minutes in a warm place. Scatter on the olives and serve with a dollop of the romesco sauce on the side.

SERVES 2

Spicy pork loin
with Thai apple salad

Pork loin is so sweet and lean and juicy. Apple traditionally goes with pork, and this salad with a zesty dressing gives the dish a crunchy Asian feel.

½ teaspoon ground cumin

½ teaspoon ground coriander

½ teaspoon ground ginger

¼ teaspoon dried chilli flakes

½ tablespoon light soy sauce

1 tablespoon sunflower oil

1 small bunch of coriander,
roots well washed and
chopped, leaves reserved

1 x 240 g pork loin

¼ cup roasted peanuts

THAI APPLE SALAD

2 Granny Smith apples, peeled
and cut into matchsticks

4 spring onions,
finely shredded

6 snow peas, finely shredded

1 stick celery, finely shredded

DRESSING

1 clove garlic, finely chopped

1 small red chilli,
finely chopped

juice of 1 lime

1 tablespoon fish sauce

1 teaspoon caster sugar

Combine the cumin, coriander, ginger, chilli flakes, soy sauce, ½ tablespoon sunflower oil and the coriander roots in a shallow dish. Add the pork loin and turn around in the spicy mixture so it is evenly coated. Leave for 15–30 minutes for the flavours to infuse.

Heat the remaining ½ tablespoon of oil in a heavy-based frying pan over a medium heat. Add the pork and cook for 5 minutes on one side, then turn and cook for another 3 minutes. Turn again and cook for 2 more minutes then remove from the pan and leave to rest in a warm place for around 5 minutes before serving. When carved, the meat should be ever so slightly pink in the centre.

To make the Thai apple salad, combine the ingredients in a mixing bowl. Mix the dressing ingredients in a small bowl and pour onto the salad. Toss so evenly coated.

To serve, arrange a mound of salad on each plate, add slices of spicy pork and sprinkle with peanuts and coriander leaves.

SERVES 2

Greek meatballs with beetroot tzatziki

See how easy it is to jazz up boring old meatballs by calling them 'Greek'? Although I love beetroot dip I don't trust those supermarket-bought ones because they're so sweet. The answer? Make your own. It's so simple.

250 g lean lamb mince

1 onion, finely chopped

½ teaspoon dried oregano

1 teaspoon chopped mint leaves

1 teaspoon chopped flat-leaf parsley leaves

1 egg, lightly beaten

juice of ½ lemon

sea salt and freshly ground pepper

½ tablespoon extra-virgin olive oil

oregano leaves

handful of small black olives

1 teaspoon toasted black sesame seeds

BEETROOT TZATZIKI

3 beetroots, heads and tails trimmed

1 whole head garlic, halved crosswise

1 tablespoon extra-virgin olive oil

½ cup Greek yoghurt

squeeze of lemon juice

salt and freshly ground pepper

To prepare the meatballs, combine all the ingredients in a bowl, except for the oil, oregano, olives and sesame seeds, and mix well. Divide into golf ball–sized portions and arrange on a tray. Cover with clingfilm and refrigerate until ready to cook.

To make the beetroot tzatziki, first preheat the oven to 200°C and line an oven tray with baking paper. Arrange the beetroots and garlic on the oven tray and drizzle with the olive oil. Roast for around 40 minutes or until tender. When cool enough to handle, rub off and discard the skins from the beetroot (wear 'sandwich' gloves so your hands don't stain) and chop them roughly. Squeeze the garlic out of its skin and combine with the chopped beetroot in a food processor. Add the yoghurt and lemon juice and season with salt and pepper. Whiz to a smooth purée.

When ready to cook the meatballs, arrange them on an oven tray lined with baking paper and drizzle with the oil. Bake for 20–25 minutes in a 180°C oven until cooked through.

Arrange the meatballs on a warmed platter and scatter on the oregano, olives and black sesame seeds. Serve with a bowl of beetroot tzatziki.

SERVES 2

Chinese chop-chop chicken

This dish came about after I experimented with dry rubs one Sunday morning. The kids could smell the chicken cooking and asked to eat it as soon as it was ready. They gave me hilarious compliments about how good it tasted and we decided that this 'Chinese chop-chop chicken' would be our new Sunday roast.

1 large organic chicken

1 tablespoon extra-virgin olive oil

CHINESE SPICE RUB

1 teaspoon fennel powder

1 teaspoon ground cinnamon

1 teaspoon ground Szechuan peppercorns

1 teaspoon ground ginger

1 teaspoon ground coriander

1 teaspoon ground cardamom

1 teaspoon turmeric

1 teaspoon 5-spice powder

1 teaspoon ground star anise

1 teaspoon sea salt

Preheat the oven to 210°C.

Mix all the spices to create a rub.

Pat the chicken dry with kitchen paper, then rub all over with olive oil. Sprinkle the spice mixture evenly over the chicken and place on an oven tray. Roast for 1 hour, or until the chicken is cooked. Check by piercing the thigh with a skewer to see if the juices run clear. Serve with steamed bok choy, tossed with a splash of sesame oil.

SERVES 4

Fish with baby tomatoes, spinach and garlic

I love Jill Dupleix; I've been reading and collecting her cookbooks for years and this is one of my favourite recipes. I've added a little twist to it by adding a splash of wine. It combines with the the garlic and tomatoes to create a delicious instant sauce.

1 x 250 g punnet cherry tomatoes

2 cloves garlic, finely sliced

2 tablespoons extra-virgin olive oil

salt and freshly ground pepper

1 x 150 g bag baby spinach leaves

2 x 120 g fillets firm white fish (rockling, orange roughie, flake)

splash of white wine

Preheat your oven to 200ºC. To make the foil bags, tear off 2 x 60 cm pieces of aluminium foil and fold each one in half.

Place the cherry tomatoes and garlic in a mixing bowl. Add the olive oil, salt and pepper and mix well. Open the pieces of foil out flat and divide the spinach between them, arranging it neatly on one side of the foil. Place the fish on top of the spinach and season with salt and pepper. Top each piece of fish with the tomato mixture then fold the foil over and scrunch the 3 open sides together leaving a slight opening at one end. Pour a splash of wine into each bag and scrunch tightly to seal. Lift the bags carefully onto an oven tray and cook for around 20 minutes.

Remove from the oven and open the bags carefully – there will be lots of hot steam. Arrange the fish on warmed plates and pour out the juices, spinach and tomatoes. Serve with an easy iceberg lettuce salad.

SERVES 2

Jane Kennedy

Rack of lamb
with gremolata crust

Gremolata is an Italian crumb mixture that combines parsley, lemon zest and garlic and adds nice touches of colour and flavour. Instead of breadcrumbs I use almond meal to create a tasty crumb crust. This dish is a bit of a splurge; it would be a good one to serve if you're having a dinner party, perhaps to follow on from Cauliflower Soup with Prawns and Chilli Oil (page 46).

100 g almond meal
1 clove garlic, crushed
large handful of flat-leaf parsley leaves
large handful of basil leaves
large handful of thyme leaves
2 tablespoons extra-virgin olive oil
1 x 6-point lamb rack (3 cutlets per person)
salt and freshly ground pepper
Dijon mustard

Preheat the oven to 200°C.

Combine the almond meal, garlic, herbs and 1 tablespoon of the oil in a food processor and whiz to combine.

Season the lamb rack with salt and pepper. Heat the remaining tablespoon of oil in a frying pan over a high heat. Add the lamb rack and sear it on all sides until evenly browned. Lift it out of the pan onto a chopping board and use a pastry brush to paint it all over with mustard. Roll the back of the rack in the crumb mixture so evenly coated and place on an oven tray. Roast for 15 minutes then remove from the oven and leave to rest in a warm place for 5–10 minutes.

When ready to serve, cut into 6 individual cutlets and serve on warmed plates.

SERVES 2

Barbecued quail with lime

I reckon you should only cook this dish if you can source butterflied quails from your poultry butcher as it is a bit fiddly trying to bone them yourself at home. Or you could ignore my advice and just cook the damn quail whole, bones and all, and lick your fingers with glee as you chew away.

1 teaspoon coriander seeds

1 teaspoon cumin seeds

2 cloves garlic, crushed

handful of coriander (including roots), roughly chopped

2 tablespoons extra-virgin olive oil

juice of 2 lemons

sea salt and freshly ground pepper

4 quails, butterflied

lime wedges

extra coriander leaves

Heat a heavy-based frying pan over a medium–high heat. Add the coriander and cumin seeds and move them around until the seeds start to pop and release their aroma. Tip into a mortar and pound to a powder then stir in the garlic, coriander, oil, lemon juice and salt and pepper.

Place the quails in a shallow dish and pour over the marinade. Turn them around in the marinade until evenly coated then cover and refrigerate for as long as you can spare. Thirty minutes is good; 1 hour is better.

Preheat the hotplate of your barbecue to high. Cook the quail, skin-side down, for around 8 minutes then turn over and cook for a further 8 minutes, or until cooked through.

Transfer the quail to a warm serving platter and sprinkle with a little more salt. Serve with lime wedges and scattered coriander leaves.

SERVES 2

Cottage pie pots

Okay, I'll be honest. I originally made these cottage pie pots for my kids. They are my take on a classic, but I've given them an 'adult' twist by topping them with creamy horseradish-flavoured cauliflower. The top goes all crunchy and cheesy.

1 tablespoon extra-virgin olive oil

½ brown onion, finely chopped

1 clove garlic, crushed

1 carrot, finely grated

400 g lean minced beef

1 tablespoon Worcestershire sauce

1 tablespoon tomato paste

salt and freshly ground pepper

400 ml salt-reduced chicken stock

sprig of rosemary, finely chopped

TOPPING

½ cauliflower, cut into florets

¼ cup skim milk

½ tablespoon Greek yoghurt

½ tablespoon horseradish cream

salt and freshly ground pepper

handful of freshly grated parmesan cheese

Preheat the oven to 180°C.

Heat the olive oil in a non-stick frying pan over a high heat. Lower the heat and add the onion, garlic and carrot to the pan. Fry for 4–5 minutes until soft and translucent. Add the minced beef to the pan and brown it slowly, stirring frequently. Add the Worcestershire sauce, tomato paste, salt and pepper and stir through. Stir in the stock and chopped rosemary and simmer for about 10 minutes, or until most of the liquid has evaporated. Remove from the heat and set aside.

To make the topping, place the cauliflower florets and milk in a microwave-safe container with a lid. Microwave on full power for 7–8 minutes, or until soft. Tip into a food processor and add the yoghurt, horseradish, salt and pepper and whiz to a smooth purée.

Divide the minced beef mixture between 4 x 250 ml ramekins then top with cauliflower purée. Sprinkle with parmesan and arrange the ramekins on an oven tray. Bake for 12–15 minutes, or until golden and bubbling. Serve immediately with salad.

SERVES 4

Takeaways

If you're ordering pizza, you're just not serious about losing weight. It's brutal, but true. **There. Is. No. Healthy. Takeaway. Food.** (Unless you are prepared to pay for home-delivered sashimi.)

If you don't cook it yourself, you get fat. It's as simple as that.

Takeaway food is very convenient – especially when it's delivered to your door. You call; they bring. But the truth is that unless you cook it yourself, you have no way of knowing exactly what ingredients you are eating – and that's the case whether you're eating food from a fancy restaurant or a fast-food joint. Many cooks don't wear the consequences of all the cream, butter, thickeners and flavour enhancers they use – we do! And what do chefs say they want to eat when they're at home? Simple food, such as omelettes or roast chicken. Join the dots!

Take it from me, you can make a really delicious, fast meal in half the time it takes for your big, fatty-boombah, cheesy, preservative-laden pizza to arrive. So chuck out your takeaway menu folder now! Here are my takes on takeaway.

Chicken san choy bau

For an even easier version of this Chinese classic, you could use a store-bought barbecued chicken.

I find a microplane grater is indispensable for getting garlic and ginger really fine and lump-free. You can find them in most good homeware stores and specialty food stores.

½ tablespoon sunflower or vegetable oil

1 tablespoon sesame oil

1 clove garlic, finely grated

1 small knob of ginger, peeled and finely grated

¼ small red chilli, finely chopped (omit seeds if cooking for kids)

2 spring onions, finely chopped

220 g chicken mince or cooked barbecued chicken, shredded

6 canned water chestnuts, chopped

½ tablespoon light soy sauce

4 iceberg lettuce leaves, chilled (make sure they are all roughly the same size)

Heat both the oils in a frying pan over a medium heat. Add the garlic, ginger, chilli and spring onions and fry for about a minute. Add the chicken mince and cook, stirring, until it loses its pink colour. If using cooked chook, simply heat it through. Stir in the water chestnuts and soy sauce, and cook briefly. Spoon into the chilled lettuce cups and serve straight away.

SERVES 2

Cos lettuce tacos

I love the taste of tacos but those corn-based shells are laden with fat. When I thought about it, I realised that what I really love about tacos is the taste of the mince with the Mexican spices combined with the crispness of the lettuce. These make a great meal or you can use baby cos lettuce leaves and serve them as a canapé.

1 tablespoon extra-virgin olive oil

350 g premium-grade beef mince

½ sachet taco seasoning

½ small red chilli, finely chopped (omit seeds if cooking for kids)

200 ml water

1 cos lettuce, leaves broken apart

2 tablespoons grated cheddar cheese

1 tomato, chopped

½ red onion, finely chopped

Heat the oil in a frying pan over a medium heat. Add the beef mince and brown it slowly, stirring frequently. Stir in the taco seasoning, chilli and water and cook for 10 minutes.

Use the cos lettuce leaves as shells and fill with the spiced mince mixture. Top with cheese, chopped tomato and a little onion.

SERVES 2

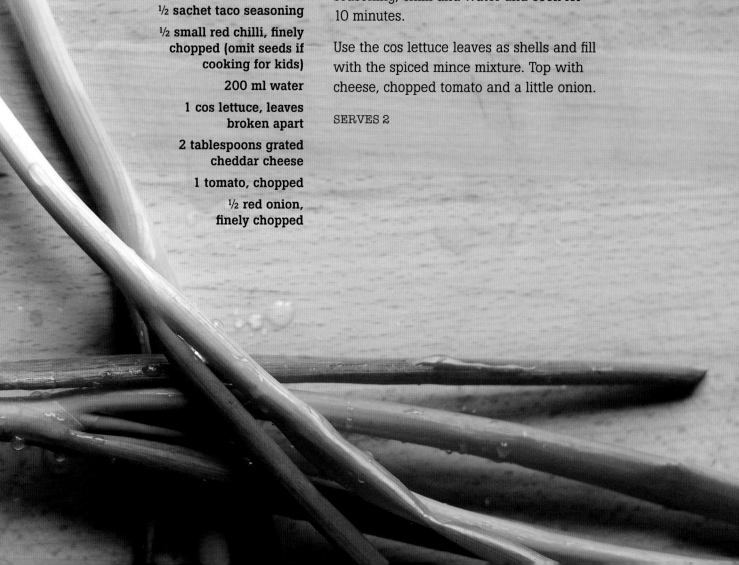

Tom yum soup in a flash

This takes about 5 minutes once you've got all your ingredients together. Sometimes I add some fresh chillies as I'm a bit of a chilli-head, but the tom yum paste is usually fiery enough. Use prawns or leftover cooked chicken – or both!

500 ml salt-reduced chicken stock

1 tablespoon tom yum paste

handful of bean sprouts

handful of chopped mushrooms

2 spring onions, chopped

2 spears asparagus, woody ends trimmed, chopped

3 snow peas, chopped

2 kaffir lime leaves, finely shredded

few prawns or some cooked chicken

1 small red chilli, chopped (optional)

handful of coriander leaves

squeeze of lime juice

Heat the stock in a saucepan then add the tom yum paste. Bring to the boil, stirring to dissolve the paste, then lower the heat and simmer for 5 minutes.

Add the vegetables, kaffir lime leaves and prawns or chicken (or both) and cook for no longer than 5 minutes. Pour into a large soup bowl and top with chilli, coriander and lime juice.

SERVES 1

Thai chicken larb with fresh accompaniments

This is a great dish for sharing and the fragrance of the herbs and lime is divine! Once you have all the ingredients prepared, it takes only minutes to cook and serve.

1 tablespoon peanut or sunflower oil

1 teaspoon sesame oil

½ red onion, finely chopped

2 cloves garlic, finely chopped

1 small knob of ginger, peeled and grated

1 small red chilli, finely chopped

2 kaffir lime leaves, finely shredded

220 g chicken mince

squeeze of lime juice

ACCOMPANIMENTS

handful of Vietnamese mint leaves, chopped

handful of coriander leaves, chopped

½ red onion, finely sliced

small handful of crushed peanuts

1 baby cos lettuce, leaves broken apart

½ continental cucumber, cut into thick strips

lime wedges

Heat both the oils in a wok or frying pan then quickly fry the onion, garlic, ginger, chilli and lime leaves over a medium heat, being careful not to burn them. Add the chicken mince and cook for around 7 minutes, stirring, until it changes colour. Add the lime juice.

Spoon into 2 bowls and top with the chopped herbs, onion slices and chopped crushed peanuts. Arrange the baby cos lettuce 'cups' and cucumber strips on a separate plate and use as scoops. Serve with lime wedges.

SERVES 2

Disorganisation is the open door through which every second excuse (or french fry) slips.

Oh no, stores are closed, better order takeaway?

Don't do it.

Tandoori chicken

I reckon I could eat this every night. The spicy Indian flavours are delicate and delicious. This version of tandoori is quick and easy and doesn't need hours of marinating. And, unlike most Indian takeaway dishes, it's *not* fattening.

2 lean chicken fillets

1 tablespoon tandoori paste

1 tablespoon Greek yoghurt

squeeze of lemon juice

few iceberg lettuce leaves, shredded

drizzle of extra-virgin olive oil

splash of red wine vinegar or lemon juice

lemon wedges

RAITA

2 tablespoons Greek yoghurt

¼ continental cucumber, seeded and finely chopped

½ tomato, seeded and finely chopped

few mint leaves, finely chopped

¼ red chilli, deseeded and finely chopped

Preheat the oven to 210°C. Line an oven tray with baking paper.

Wrap the chicken fillets in clingfilm and use a rolling pin or heavy can to bash them flat. Don't be too vigorous – you don't want them to fall apart. Cut each fillet into around 3 pieces.

In a mixing bowl, combine the tandoori paste, yoghurt and lemon juice. Add the chicken pieces and mix with the marinade until well coated. Cover with clingfilm and refrigerate for 10 minutes for the flavours to infuse.

When ready to cook, place the chicken on the oven tray and cook for 25–30 minutes, or until the chicken is cooked through.

To make the raita, combine all ingredients and refrigerate until ready to serve.

Toss the shredded lettuce with the olive oil and vinegar (or lemon juice). Serve the chicken with the salad, lemon wedges and raita.

SERVES 2

Seafood green curry

I absolutely love Thai food, but unfortunately many dishes are very fattening, thanks to the amount of coconut milk used – especially in Thai curries. I spent ages trying to crack the code on this one, and I reckon this recipe works. I use a tiny amount of light coconut milk, but still manage to get that Thai green curry taste. If you prefer to use chicken instead of seafood, go ahead!

1 tablespoon peanut oil

8 green prawns, cleaned, shelled, deveined, tails intact

1 x 150 g piece blue eye or rockling, cut into large chunks

1 onion, cut into chunks

1 clove garlic, chopped

1 small red chilli, finely chopped

2 teaspoons Thai green curry paste

handful of green beans

¼ cup light coconut milk

250 ml salt-reduced chicken stock

juice of ½ lime

2 kaffir lime leaves, finely shredded

1 zucchini, sliced

6 mussels, scrubbed

1 tablespoon coriander or basil leaves

Heat ½ tablespoon of the oil in a non-stick frying pan over a high heat. Add the prawns and fry for about 2 minutes until they turn pink. Transfer the prawns to a bowl and set aside.

Add the fish pieces and fry over a high heat for 2–3 minutes, or until just cooked. Transfer to the same bowl as the prawns. Cover with aluminium foil to keep warm.

Lower the heat slightly and pour in the remaining oil. Add the onion, garlic, chilli and curry paste and fry for around 2 minutes. Be careful, it will spit! Add the beans to the pan and toss in the spice paste for another minute. Reduce the heat to low and add the coconut milk, chicken stock, lime juice, kaffir lime leaves and zucchini. Simmer for 30 seconds then return the seafood to the pan and add the mussels. Simmer for around 5 minutes, or until the mussels have opened (discard any that remain closed).

Ladle into warm bowls. Chop the herbs at the last minute and sprinkle onto the curry as you serve.

SERVES 2

Satay chicken with peanut sauce, pineapple, and cucumber salad

This is a lower calorie version of one of my favourites. The sauce is made fresh and doesn't come from a jar of full-fat peanut sauce and sugar. These satays are best cooked using bamboo skewers. Just remember to soak them in water for 20 minutes before cooking, to stop them burning.

2 tablespoons Greek yoghurt

2 cloves garlic, chopped

½ teaspoon ground cumin

¼ teaspoon chilli powder

½ teaspoon ground coriander

½ teaspoon salt

3 skinless chicken fillets, cut into strips

few slices of fresh pineapple, chopped

¼ small white onion, finely chopped

PEANUT DIPPING SAUCE

¼ cup sugar-free peanut butter

¼ cup water

½ clove garlic

1 tablespoon lime juice

1 tablespoon light soy sauce

½ teaspoon caster sugar

pinch of chilli or cayenne pepper

CUCUMBER SALAD

1 Lebanese cucumber, peeled and sliced into discs

½ cup water

2 tablespoons white vinegar

1 small red chilli, deseeded and finely chopped

In a mixing bowl, combine the yoghurt, garlic, cumin, chilli powder, coriander and salt. Add the chicken strips and mix with the marinade until well coated. Cover with clingfilm and refrigerate for 10 minutes for the flavours to infuse.

To make the peanut sauce, combine all the ingredients in a blender and whiz until smooth. Cover and refrigerate until ready to serve.

To make the salad, toss the cucumber with the water, vinegar and chilli and refrigerate for about 20 minutes.

When ready to cook, preheat the oven to 180°C and line an oven tray with baking paper. Scrape most of the marinade off the chicken then thread the pieces onto presoaked bamboo skewers. Arrange on the oven tray and cook for 15–20 minutes.

Serve the satays with the chopped pineapple, onion, cucumber salad and the peanut dipping sauce.

SERVES 4

My beef vindaloo

This is one of my greatest triumphs. I had this recipe analysed in a food laboratory and then compared to takeaway beef vindaloo. The results show that my dish has:

Less than HALF the fat

Less than HALF the cholesterol

And only 60% of the calories of takeaway beef vindaloos.

Gotta be happy with that.

As this curry is slow-cooked it makes a great weekend dish.

2 tablespoons sunflower oil
1 onion, sliced
1 kg stewing steak, cut into cubes
2 cloves garlic, chopped
1 knob of ginger, peeled and chopped
2 teaspoons ground coriander
½ teaspoon ground turmeric
500 ml salt-reduced chicken stock
1 x 400 g can chopped tomatoes

SPICE PASTE
1 tablespoon cumin seeds
1½ teaspoons black mustard seeds
1 teaspoon peppercorns
1 teaspoon fenugreek seeds
1 teaspoon cardamom seeds
1 teaspoon ground cinnamon
4 dried red chillies
½ teaspoon salt
1 teaspoon brown sugar
5 tablespoons white wine vinegar

To make the spice paste, combine the cumin, mustard seeds, peppercorns, fenugreek, cardamom, cinnamon and chillies in a spice grinder and whiz to a powder (or use a mortar and pestle). Add the salt, sugar and vinegar and stir to a paste. Transfer to a blender.

Heat 1 tablespoon oil in a large frying pan over a low–medium heat. Add the onion and fry until golden. Tip into the blender with the spice paste and whiz to a thick paste. Set aside.

To cook the beef, heat the remaining oil in a large ovenproof saucepan or flameproof casserole dish. Brown the beef in batches, then remove with a slotted spoon and set aside. Add the garlic and ginger to the pan and cook for 2 minutes. Add the ground coriander and turmeric and fry for a further 2 minutes. Add the spice paste and cook over low heat for 5 minutes. Stir in the stock and tomatoes return the beef to the pan. Cover with a lid and cook for 1½ hours, or until the beef is very tender.

Serve with Cauliflower 'Rice' (page 151) and Raita (page 137).

SERVES 4

Jane Kennedy

Sides

As you've been flicking through this book, you will have probably noticed that there is an obvious lack of carbohydrate-based foods. I try not to indulge in high-carb foods because they **MAKE ME FAT**.

In this chapter I'd like to show you how – particularly with your evening meal – you can enjoy many different types of filling vegetable-based side dishes, without thinking you have to resort to the standard stodge. Enjoy!

Cauliflower 'rice'

You know how rice has the ability to soak up delicious juices? Well, rice is not happening in this cookbook. But please try this dish whenever you really think you're missing out – it goes beautifully with My Beef Vindaloo (page 144), or any Thai dish in this book, or even the Moroccan Chicken Tagine (page 88).

I know it sounds weird, but I promise you it works.

½ **cauliflower**

Pull the cauliflower apart into small florets and place in a microwave-safe container with a lid. Do not add water. Microwave on full power for 5 minutes.

Using a hand-held blender, whiz the cauliflower until it starts to resemble rice. Alternatively, pulse it in bursts in a food processor. This is all it needs. Serve immediately.

SERVES 2

Spanish mushrooms with thyme

I love Spanish food, and this dish is one of my favourites. If you can, use one of those Spanish terracotta serving dishes. Serve it really hot, straight from the oven, so the mushrooms are bubbling as you bring them to the table.

1 tablespoon extra-virgin olive oil

1 teaspoon butter

1 clove garlic, finely chopped

500 g button mushrooms or similar

splash of white wine

few sprigs of thyme

juice of ½ lemon

1 tablespoon yoghurt

salt and freshly ground pepper

Preheat the oven to 200ºC.

Combine all the ingredients in a terracotta or similar ovenproof dish and cook for 15–20 minutes, or until you can see the mushrooms bubbling. Serve immediately.

SERVES 2

Asparagus in lemon and olive oil

You can also cook this dish on a barbecue or griddle plate. It is an easy accompaniment to meat, chicken or fish.

10 spears asparagus, woody ends trimmed
glug of extra-virgin olive oil
squeeze of lemon juice
salt and freshly ground pepper

Place the asparagus spears in a flat bowl. Add the olive oil, lemon juice, salt and pepper and turn them around so evenly coated. Leave for 10 minutes – which is about the time it takes to cook and rest a piece of chicken or steak.

Heat a frying pan or griddle plate over a high heat. Add the asparagus with its marinade and cook for 3 minutes, tossing and turning with tongs, until just tender. Serve straight away.

SERVES 2

Broccolini with garlic and almonds

1 bunch broccolini
1 tablespoon extra-virgin olive oil
1 ½ cloves garlic, thinly sliced
¼ cup slivered almonds, lightly toasted
sea salt and freshly ground pepper
lemon wedges

Cook the broccolini in a large saucepan of lightly salted boiling water for about 2 minutes. Drain well.

Heat the oil in a frying pan over a medium heat. Add the garlic and fry for around 30 seconds. Add the almonds and broccolini to the pan and toss in the oil. Season with salt and pepper and stir over the heat for another minute. Serve immediately with lemon wedges.

SERVES 2

Share meals, talk over recipes …
Inspire each other!

Tastiest tomatoes with sea salt and olive oil

Anyone from the Mediterranean will have a good old laugh at seeing this included as a 'recipe', but sometimes the simplest dishes are the ones you forget about. I love this dish so much that I serve it nearly every night. I am very fussy with tomatoes and I don't think I'm the only one, so I insist that you source the very best cherry tomatoes you can. Do *not* store these babies in the fridge.

12 cherry tomatoes, halved (at room temperature)

sea salt

1½ tablespoons best-quality extra-virgin olive oil

small handful of flat-leaf parsley leaves

few basil leaves

¼ red onion, finely chopped

Arrange the tomatoes on a plate. Sprinkle with sea salt and drizzle on the olive oil.

Leave to rest for about 10 minutes.

Just before serving, chop the parsley and basil leaves finely. Scatter the onion over the tomatoes then top with the chopped herbs.

SERVES 2

Crunchy beans with anchovy and goat's cheese dressing

This side dish goes with everything. Don't be freaked out by the anchovies; they dissolve in the dressing, leaving only a gorgeous salty flavour.

400 g long green beans

4 anchovy fillets, rinsed and finely chopped

1 shallot, finely chopped

1 tablespoon extra-virgin olive oil

2 teaspoons lemon juice

sea salt and freshly ground pepper

60 g marinated goat's cheese, crumbled

¼ cup pine nuts, lightly toasted

Bring a large saucepan of salted water to the boil. Add the beans and blanch for 1 minute. Drain the beans well then tip them into a bowl of cold water, which preserves the colour and stops them cooking any further.

Combine the anchovies, shallot, olive oil and lemon juice in a mixing bowl. Season to taste with salt and pepper. Arrange the beans on a serving platter and drizzle on the dressing. Toss gently then top with the crumbled goat's cheese and toasted pine nuts and serve.

SERVES 4

Savoy cabbage

I prefer savoy cabbage to regular cabbage when cooked and served hot. It's fabulous with pork fillet or even with a rack of lamb. It's very easy to cook, too. Just shred half a cabbage finely and blanch it in boiling salted water for 30 seconds. Drain thoroughly, then pan-fry for 1 minute with a teaspoon of butter and salt and pepper. If you are in a bold mood, pan-fry 1 rasher of finely chopped lean bacon, and toss through the cabbage just before serving.

SERVES 2

Balsamic baby onions

The natural sugars in the onions combine with the balsamic vinegar to create a wonderful sticky coating. This is a bit of an indulgence, but the onions make the perfect accompaniment to a good piece of steak.

10 white pearl onions

1 tablespoon extra-virgin olive oil

sea salt and freshly ground pepper

2 tablespoons balsamic vinegar

¼ cup salt-reduced chicken stock

1 teaspoon butter

1 teaspoon chopped rosemary leaves

Bring a large saucepan of water to the boil and cook the onions for 1 minute with their skins on. Remove the onions with a slotted spoon and leave to cool a little. When cool enough to handle, peel the skins away and discard them.

Place the onions in a mixing bowl and add the olive oil and salt and pepper and toss so they are well coated.

Heat a non-stick frying pan on a medium–high heat. Sauté the onions for about 5 minutes until they start to colour a lovely golden brown. Lower the heat and add the balsamic vinegar and the stock. Cover the pan and simmer for about 10 minutes, or until the onions are tender.

Remove the lid from the pan, add the butter and rosemary and cook for around 2 minutes until the liquid has reduced a little. Jiggle the pan continuously to keep the onions coated in the sticky sauce. Pour the onions onto a platter and serve.

SERVES 2

Desserts

I have to say I'm not all that big on dessert, as I have a more savoury palate. So this is a very 'skinny' chapter. But I do understand that there are plenty of people with a sweet tooth that needs to be satisfied. So, if you simply must have a touch of sweetness, here are a few dessert suggestions that taste delicious and are a perfect way to end a meal.

You'll see that most of my desserts are based around fresh fruit – don't even think about opening a can of fruit with all that sugary, heavy syrup. Over the years I've done a bit experimenting and the natural sugars in most fruits are sweet enough on their own without the need to add any sugar. With this in mind, treat yourself to the ripest, juiciest and sweetest fruit you can find.

Apple and lemon snow

My grandmother used to make this when my sister and I were little and I remember how much we loved it. I really don't think you need to add any sugar, especially if you choose naturally sweet apples, but if you really *must* add sugar, then 1 teaspoon of caster sugar whisked into the egg whites should do it. This dessert looks fabulous served in a chilled glass.

4 apples (fuji or pink lady), peeled and sliced

2 tablespoons water

2 large egg whites

zest of 1 lemon, some reserved to garnish

4 small mint leaves

Place the apples in a saucepan with the water. Bring to the boil, then lower the heat and simmer, covered, until the apples are very soft. If you're in a real hurry, you could microwave the apples in a microwave-safe container for approximately 10 minutes on full power. But be careful as the apples will be really hot. Drain the cooked apples then whiz them to a purée in a blender or food processor and leave to cool. When cool, refrigerate until chilled.

Whisk the egg whites to form stiff peaks, as if making meringue. Gently fold in the apple purée and lemon zest. Divide the mixture between 4 chilled glasses and return to the fridge until ready to serve. Top with a mint leaf and a little more lemon zest.

SERVES 4

Grilled peaches

Clearly this will be a seasonal dessert and you'll know
just the right time to choose those gorgeous soft ripe
peaches … white, yellow, whichever you like. Of course,
nectarines will work just as well. The natural sugars
are released once the peaches hit the pan or grill
and caramelise.

4 peaches
1 tablespoon balsamic vinegar
4 teaspoons Greek yoghurt

Heat a griddle or barbecue.

Cut the peaches in half and remove the
stones. There is no need to peel them.
Place the peaches flesh-side down and
cook for approximately 3 minutes or until
the fruit has a nice brown colour.

To serve, drizzle with balsamic vinegar and
a dollop of yoghurt.

SERVES 4

Fresh pineapple and mint

I first saw this idea in a Jamie Oliver cookbook, and it made me realise how well herbs and fruit go together. This is another refreshing dessert that relies on the natural sweetness of the pineapple, so make sure it's ripe. And look, I even add a teaspoon of sugar!

½ **ripe pineapple, peeled**
1 cup mint leaves
1 teaspoon sugar

Cut the pineapple into very fine slices and arrange them on a platter, carpaccio style.

Roughly smash the mint leaves using a mortar and pestle, then mix in the sugar. Sprinkle the minty mixture over the pineapple and serve.

SERVES 2

Strawberries in balsamic with Greek yoghurt

This has been a staple dessert in our house since the 1980s and I still love this way of serving strawberries.

250 g strawberries, hulled
1 tablespoon balsamic vinegar
2 tablespoons Greek yoghurt

Place the strawberries in a large mixing bowl. Drizzle with the vinegar and mix gently. Divide between 4 dessert bowls and serve each with a dollop of yoghurt.

SERVES 4

Strawberry granita

I tried a number of different ways to make a frozen, refreshing strawberry dessert. After a few disasters, this is what I came up with. Trust me, it wasn't rocket science in the end.

The only ingredient in this dish is … strawberries! In which case I think it's vital you find the sweetest, most luscious strawberries you can.

500 g strawberries

Tip the strawberries into a blender or food processor and whiz to a smooth purée (or use a hand-held blender). Pour into a rectangular container and freeze. Every few hours, remove from the freezer and beat lightly with a fork to mix in the frozen crystals. By the time it is frozen firm, the granita should be quite granular with small, icy crystals. Remove from the freezer 10–15 minutes before serving. It looks best served in glasses or round glass bowls.

SERVES 4

Nashi pear with lime juice

Thank you to Charles at the Japanese restaurant Jamon for this dessert idea.

Cut a cold, ripe nashi pear into bite-sized pieces. No need to peel. Squeeze on a little fresh lime juice, spear each piece with a toothpick and serve!

SERVES 1

Walnuts with celery, pear and brie

. . . .

I'm a self-confessed cheese-head and this is my 'fix' when I need something extra after dinner. You have to be very strong and only allow yourself one piece of brie, and I say eat it with a knife and fork, as the French do, so that once you're finished, you're *finished*. Get it?

piece of the most delectable brie you can afford

½ nice firm pear

few walnuts

few celery leaves

I like to arrange this beautifully – as if serving an entrée. Cut a wedge from the brie and place it on an attractive plate. Arrange a few slices of the pear to one side and scatter on the walnuts and celery leaves.

SERVES 1

Acknowledgements

Thank you to the ever-chic, professional and positive publisher extraordinaire Mary Small; we were always on the same page. Thank you for making this experience such a treat. Thanks also to Ellie Smith for your warmth and considered input. Mark Roper, your photos look good enough to eat and are ever so fancy. Trisha Garner, I love your design; thanks for helping so much of me morph its way into the book. Leesa O'Reilly, wow, you have beautiful taste! Deb Kaloper, thank you for your really lovely food styling ... who knew my dishes could look like that? Mara Szoeke and Michele Curtis, I was thrilled with the way you prepared the dishes, and learned a lot along the way ... thank you. Also thanks to Lucy Malouf for sound and helpful editing.

Sandy Grant, thanks again for being so cool, calm and collected in supporting my first foray into the cook book world. Donna Aston, you're so inspiring and you've helped me change the way I think and look at food and exercise. Thank you. Sandra and Belinda, I couldn't have done this without you; thank you both so much. Tom, Santo, Rob and Hirshy ... you are my mentors and friends. Thanks for all your love, encouragement and support over the past 20 years.

Index